Rum & Reggae's Puerto Rico

Including Culebra & Vieques

Rum&Reggae®'s

Puerto Rico

Including Culebra & Vieques

SECOND EDITION

written and edited by

Jonathan Runge
& Adam Carter

Rum & Reggae Guidebooks, Inc.
Boston, Massachusetts • August 2007

Copyright © 2007 by Rum & Reggae Guidebooks, Inc.

All rights reserved under International and Pan-American Copyright Conventions.

Published in the United States by Rum & Reggae Guidebooks, Inc., Boston, MA. All rights reserved. No part of this book may be used or reproduced in any manner whatsoever without written permission except in the case of brief quotations embodied in critical articles or reviews. For information, contact Rum & Reggae Guidebooks, Inc., P.O. Box 130153, Boston, MA 02113.

Rum & Reggae® and Travel with an Opinion® are trademarks of Rum & Reggae Guidebooks, Inc.

Second Edition

ISBN: 978-1-893675-15-5
ISSN: 1557-9220

Edited by Jonathan Runge

Co-edited by Joe Shapiro

Book design by Valerie Brewster, Scribe Typography
Cover design by Jonathan Runge and Valerie Brewster

Illustrations by Eric Orner

Front Cover Photo of Playa Crash Boat by Ramón Morales of Welcome to Rincón.com, www.welcometorincon.com

Back Cover Photos: Faro de Arecibo by Jorge Collazo at www.PhotosofPuertoRico .com and www.fotografiapr.com; Playa Flamenco by Fotosearch at www.fotosearch.com

Maps by Shane Matthews of Full View Mapping

Printed in the United States

For Kyle

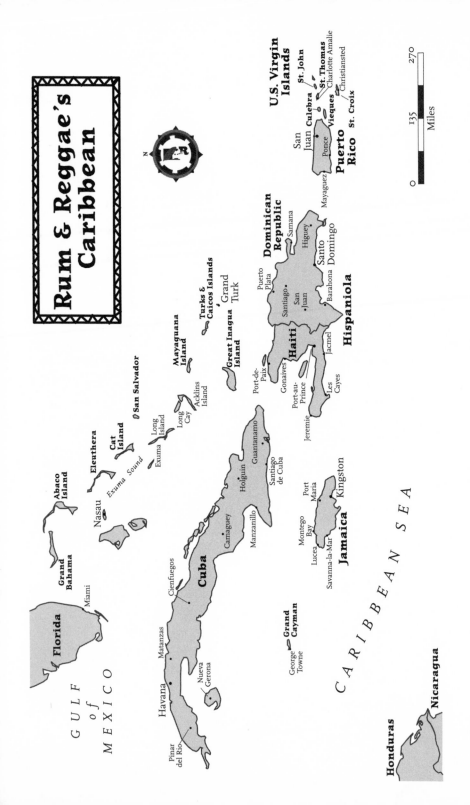

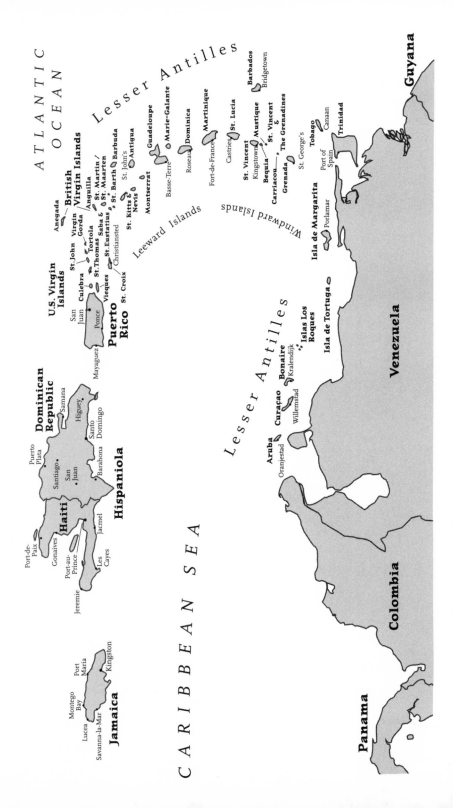

CONTENTS

Before You Go 3

Puerto Rico 17 TOURISTO SCALE: 👤👤👤👤👤👤👤👤👤 (9)

San Juan 25

Don't Miss

Culebra 113   TOURISTO SCALE: 🐵🐵🐵 (3)

Don't Miss

Vieques 127   TOURISTO SCALE: 🐵🐵🐵🐵 (4)

Don't Miss

INDEX OF MAPS

Lodging and Restaurant Key

Note: We have used a number of symbols and terms to indicate prices and ambiance. Here are the code breakers.

Lodging Symbols

ⓒ telephone number

✆ fax number

💻 Web site URL and/or e-mail address

💲 room rates

🍴 meal plan

[CC] major credit cards
Visa, Master Card, and usually American Express and Discover

★ This is a Rum & Reggae "best of category" establishment.

Lodging Rates

- Prices are rack rates for the least expensive double (two people) in high season — generally mid-December through mid-April — unless otherwise noted. Off-season rates are often as much as 50 percent cheaper. Unless otherwise noted, prices for singles are the same or slightly less.

Dirt Cheap	under $50
Cheap	$51–$100
Not So Cheap	$101–$150
Pricey	$151–$200
Very Pricey	$201–$300
Wicked Pricey	$301–$400
Ridiculous	$401–$500
Beyond Belief	$501–$600
Stratospheric	$601 and up!

- Expect a service and tax charge (and, in some cases, resort fee) of at least 15 percent added to your bill. Some places can reach 25 percent! Ouch! Be sure to ask ahead of time to avoid going into shock. (Don't hesitate to ask at the front desk how the service charge will be distributed to employees — sometimes you are not expected to leave any additional tips.)

- Be sure to ask about credit cards when making your reservations if you intend to use them for payment. A few places, even expensive ones, do not accept credit cards.

- Hotels in *Rum & Reggae's Puerto Rico* are listed in order of what we recommend most to what we recommend least (within each town or neighborhood), regardless of rates. By doing this, we avoid the practice of listing hotels solely in order of rates, which often serves to bury the lower-priced hotels at the bottom of the list.

Lodging and Meal Codes ⑪

All hotel prices are assigned a corresponding code that relates to the meals that are included in the rates.

EP   **European Plan** — No meals included.

CP   **Continental Plan** — Continental breakfast (bread, cereal, juice, coffee) included.

BP   **Breakfast Plan** — Full hot breakfast included.

MAP   **Modified American Plan** — Full breakfast and dinner included.

FAP   **Full American Plan** — Full breakfast, lunch, and dinner included (sometimes with an afternoon "tea" or snack as well).

All-Inclusive   All meals, beer, wine, and well drinks (house brands) are included, most or all on-site activities, and usually tax and service charges.

Restaurant Prices

Prices represent per-person cost for the average meal, from soup to nuts. Restaurants are separated by neighborhood (where applicable) and are listed alphabetically.

$	Under $15	$$$$	$36–$50
$$	$15–$25	$$$$$	Over $50
$$$	$26–$35		

Touristo Scale 🕵

You'll find the key to our Touristo Scale on the last page of the book.

ACKNOWLEDGMENTS

Contrary to what you might think, writing a book on the Caribbean is not very glamorous. The most glamorous part about doing it is answering the "So what do you do?" question at cocktail parties. It's all uphill from there. We did not spend our days on the beach or by the pool sipping a piña colada. Well, okay, sometimes we did. But most of the time we were running around checking out this or that and complaining about the heat. Just when we started to get comfortable in one place, it was time to uproot ourselves and start all over again. Try doing that every other day and you'll begin to know what we mean.

Fortunately, some wonderful people helped us out along the way. We'd like to take this opportunity to sincerely thank those who did. In no particular order, they are Suzanne Adams, Linda and Burr Vail, Concepción Cano, Leana and Enrique Ducournau, Celia Ross, Gaia Peri, Simonique Jack, Harold Davies and Kingsley Wratten, Wilhelm Sack, Mark Browne, Andres Branger, Diane Lulek, Laura Davidson, Kim Greiner, Luana Wheatley, Cheryl Andrews, Margie Benziger, Lisa Blau, Molly Tichy, Gerald Hill, Roberta Garzaroli, Muriel Wiltord, Guy-Claude Germain, Glenn C. Holm, Roland Lopes, Elise Magras, Helen Kidd, Cristina Rivas, Marilyn Marx, Angela Sinto, Leslie Cohen, Marie Kephart, Melanie Brandman and Associates, Jodie Diamond, Janelle James, Kara Barbakoff, Marie Rosa, Cathy Preece, Melissa Lukis, Shantini Ramakrishnan, Barbara Walker and Shireen Aga, Matthew Snow, Erika Vives, Andria Mitsakos, Katie Rogers, and Gay Myers. If we overlooked your name, sorry, but thanks for your help!

Rum & Reggae's Puerto Rico, Including Culebra & Vieques is published by Rum & Reggae Guidebooks, Inc. We are not exactly an industry behemoth, but we have many helpers, and all deserve hearty thanks. Our warmest gratitude goes to the following: our fabulous and wonderfully easygoing book designer, Valerie Brewster of Scribe

Typography; our very talented Web designer, Michael Carlson; our corporate illustrator and Disney animation megastar, Eric Orner; our cartographer, Shane Matthews of Full View Mapping; our very supportive distributor, Independent Publishers Group—its chief, Curt Matthews, the tireless Mary Rowles, and the rest of its great staff; our legal team at Sheehan, Phinney, Bass & Green of Maria Recalde and Doug Verge; our printer, McNaughton & Gunn; and our patient copy editor and indexer, Judith Antonelli.

There were several people who helped in other ways. Many thanks to Lynn Clark, Dorothy Shapiro, Jordan Shapiro, Gail Shapiro, Andy Shapiro, Ruth Bonsignore, Kevin Moore, Duncan Donahue and Tom Fortier, Nan Garland, Elvis Jiménez-Chávez and Chris Lawrence, Bucky Parker, Brendan Hickey and Judith Wright, Martin Merle, Matt Wilhelm, Megan McElheran, Nicole Riddle and the rest of the Stanford gang, David Swanson, and Tony Lulek. Adam sends a special thanks to his father, Allan Carter, for teaching him to write; his mother, Linda Champagne, for inspiring him to help others; and his global cohort, Laz, for helping him to expand his mind through years of international trailblazing. Finally, a wicked thanks to Rum & Reggae's president, Joe Shapiro, whose enthusiasm, dedication, and hard work helped to push this book to completion.

As always, a can of dolphin-safe tuna to the Rum & Reggae cat and guardian angel, Jada.

To all who helped, many thanks—YAH MON!

Jonathan Runge and Adam Carter
Co-Authors
Rum & Reggae Guidebooks, Inc.
Boston, Massachusetts
August 1, 2007

WRITE TO RUM & REGGAE

Dear *Rum & Reggae's Puerto Rico* Readers,

We really do appreciate and value your comments, suggestions, or information about anything new or exciting in Puerto Rico and the rest of the Caribbean. We'd love to hear about your experiences, good and bad, while you were there. Your feedback will help us to shape future editions. So please let us hear from you.

Visit our Web site at www.rumreggae.com, e-mail us at yahmon @rumreggae.com, or write to:

Mr. Yah Mon
Rum & Reggae Guidebooks
P.O. Box 130153
Boston, MA 02113

Sincerely,

Joe Shapiro
President

P.S. We often mention cocktails, drinking, and other things in this book. We certainly do not mean to upset any nondrinkers or those in recovery. Please don't take offense—rum and its relatives are not a requirement for a successful vacation in the Caribbean.

INTRODUCTION

Travel with an Opinion®. That's how we describe our distinct point of view. *Rum & Reggae's Puerto Rico* is not your typical tourist guide to the Isle of Enchantment. We like to say that the Rum & Reggae series is written for people who want more out of a vacation than the standard tourist fare. Our reader is sophisticated and independent. He's also more lively — be it exploring, beaching, hiking, sailing, windsurfing, golfing, scuba diving, festivities seeking, or just pure partying. Or she's more particular, in search of places that are secluded, cerebral, or spiritual.

This book differs from other guidebooks in another way. Instead of telling you that everything is "nice" — nice, that is, for the average Joe and Jane — *Rum & Reggae's Puerto Rico* offers definitive opinions. We will tell you what's fantastic and what's not, from the point of view of someone who loathes the tourist label and the other bland and tired travel books whose names we won't mention.

We'll take you all over Puerto Rico, Culebra, and Vieques while sharing our recommendations of where to go (and where not to go). More important, we filter out all the crap for you so you can have fun reading the book and enjoy your vacation and keep the decision making to a minimum.

So mix yourself a piña colada (don't forget to use fresh pineapple juice), put on some salsa, and sit back and let *Rum & Reggae's Puerto Rico* take you on your own private voyage to *las islas bonitas.*

Rum & Reggae's Puerto Rico

Including Culebra & Vieques

Before You Go

Calling Puerto Rico, Culebra, and Vieques

In planning your trip, you're likely to make a few phone calls to the destinations you'll be visiting. Just to be clear, Puerto Rico, Culebra, and Vieques are all part of the United States, so when calling these islands, you can simply dial the same as you would when calling from one state to another in the United States.

English Spoken Here?

Some visitors are concerned about their inability to speak Spanish, but rest assured, English is widely spoken throughout these three islands, particularly within establishments like hotels and restaurants that cater to tourists. However, it's always fun to toss around a few words or phrases, so feel free to refer to our Spanish Survival Guide (in the back of this book) for those rare occasions when you encounter folks who don't speak English.

Passport Formalities

Since this is the United States, U.S. citizens do not need to present passports or birth certificates when traveling between the mainland and Puerto Rico, Culebra, or Vieques. It's just like traveling from one U.S. state to another. However, due to airport security, it is necessary to carry a government-issued photo ID (e.g., a driver's license) prior to boarding a plane. Non–U.S. citizens should follow the same entry requirements as if they were entering any other part of the United States. In other words, if foreign visitors (including Canadian citizens) are arriving by air from a non–U.S. destination, they should carry a passport (or visa, if necessary). Citizens of Britain and other Visa Waiver Program (VWP) countries can enter without visas if their passports conform to certain specific requirements of the U.S. government. For example, citizens of VWP countries who hold e-passports—and, depending upon their date of issue, some passports with digital photos printed on the data page—and passports with machine-readable zones might not need a visa. For information on more specific entry requirements, check with the U.S. Department of State Web site before traveling: www.travel.state.gov.

About Money

The unit of currency is the U.S. dollar. ATMs are plentiful, but non–U.S. citizens should keep in mind that it might be hard to find places to exchange currency in the rural parts of Puerto Rico, Culebra, and Vieques.

Climate

The weather in Puerto Rico, Culebra, and Vieques is about as close to perfect as anywhere on Earth. The temperature rarely dips below 70°F or scales to above 90°F (at sea level). It can get cooler at night in the mountains, making it ideal for sleeping. The sun shines almost every day. Rainfall comes in the form of brief, intense cloudbursts, quickly followed by sunshine. It's pretty hard not to get a tan.

The reasons for this ideal climate are the constant temperature of the ocean—about 80°F year-round—and the steady trade winds from Africa. The Caribbean is not susceptible to the harsh weather patterns of the middle latitudes. The only weather peril of a Caribbean vacation is an occasional summer tropical depression or hurricane, which can make life very exciting.

There are two basic climate categories in Puerto Rico: lush (very green, hot, somewhat humid, with lots of rainfall) and arid (brown with cactus and very dry). The windward side (the north and east coasts) is the lush, wetter, and greener side. The mountains that traverse the center of the island from east to west, the Cordillera Central, block most of the typical rainfall that comes with the prevailing trade winds. This makes the southern and western coasts semi-arid to arid. A striking example of this contrast is readily seen with the drive on Route 52 from San Juan to Ponce. The change from verdant to brown happens in just a few miles once the summit of the road is passed.

Culebra and Vieques are very arid islands, due to the lack of mountains to catch the clouds and rainfall. Vegetation is scrubby with cactus, although there certainly are enough palm trees to keep palm tree lovers happy.

Both lush and arid climes are warm to hot, depending on the season and the extent of the trade winds. Summer, while only a few degrees hotter than winter, feels much warmer due to the increased humidity and decreased wind. The one constant is the sun. It is always strong and will swiftly fry unprotected pale faces — and bodies — to a glowing shade of lobster red.

A Note to Our Gay and Lesbian Readers

Travel to the Caribbean should be an enjoyable and wonderful experience for all, and it usually is. Though not as relaxed as St. Barth, Martinique, or Guadeloupe, Puerto Rico, Culebra, and Vieques have a welcoming attitude toward homosexuality (keep in mind that San Juan can have typical big-city safety issues).

Most gays and lesbians never encounter problems related to homophobia in their travels around the Caribbean, but we have been informed of a few incidents that give us pause and warrant this alert. So when in unfamiliar environments, please use good judgment and common sense. We value everyone's safety more than making political or social statements. Please keep this in mind should your itinerary find you continuing on to some of the other islands, such as the former and current British colonies — they are not as socially accepting of gay and lesbian relationships as in certain enlightened parts of the United States, Canada, and Britain. In fact, some islands, especially Jamaica, are very homophobic (see www.glaad.org for more information), with a very conservative Christian value system. That said, many gay and lesbian travelers go anywhere and everywhere, and we would never discourage anyone from seeking adventure and fun.

What to Wear and Take Along

Less is more. That is always the motto to remember when packing to go to the Caribbean. Bring only what you can carry for 10 minutes at a good clip, because you'll often be schlepping your luggage for at least that time, and it's hot. Rollerboards—that is, luggage with wheels—are handy, although you'll still have to check (or gate-check) them on many of the smaller planes.

What you really need to take along are a bathing suit, shorts, T-shirts or tanks, a cotton sweater, a pair of sandals, sunglasses, and an iPod. After all, you are on vacation. However, this is the new millennium and people are dressing up for no reason, so you might want to bring some extra togs to look presentable at the dinner table. To help you be totally prepared (and to make your packing a lot easier), we've assembled a list of essentials for a week.

The Packing List

Clothes

- [ ] bathing suit (or two)
- [ ] T-shirts (4)—you'll end up buying at least one
- [ ] tank tops (2)—they're cooler, show off your muscles or curves, and even out T-shirt tan lines
- [ ] polo shirts (2)
- [ ] shorts (2)
- [ ] nice, compatible lightweight pants (also good for the plane)
- [ ] sandals—those that can get wet, like Tevas, are best
- [ ] cotton sweater or sweatshirt (if traveling in the winter)
- [ ] undergarments
- [ ] sneakers (or good walking shoes) or topsiders (for boaters)
- [ ] Women: lightweight dress (most women prefer to bring a couple of dresses for evening)

☐ Men: if you must have a lightweight sport coat, wear it (with appropriate shoes) on the plane

Essentials

☐ toiletries and any necessary meds

☐ sunscreen or sunblock (SPF 15+ and lip protector)

☐ moisturizer

☐ pure aloe gel for sunburn

☐ some good books — don't count on finding a worthwhile read outside the city

☐ Cutter's or Woodsman's insect repellent, or Skin So Soft (oh, those nasty bugs)

☐ sunglasses (we bring two pairs!)

☐ hat or visor

☐ iPod

☐ camcorder, digital camera, or pocket camera (disposables are great for the beach, and underwater disposables for snorkeling)

Sports Accessories (where applicable)

☐ tennis racket

☐ golf clubs

☐ hiking shoes

☐ fins, mask, snorkel, regulator/BC, and C-card (certification card)

Documents

☐ ATM card and credit cards

☐ valid passport for non–U.S. citizens (keep in hotel safe and carry around a photocopy in your wallet)

☐ driver's license

Flying the Caribbean Way

If you are traveling only to and from Puerto Rico, you'll probably be flying on a major carrier. However, if you plan to travel to some of the other islands in the region (as we always seem to do), chances are you'll be flying on one or more of the regional carriers (below). Although we've had many faultless experiences, we've also had a few hiccups along the way. Having flown local island carriers extensively, we've developed some golden rules for stress-free flying when in the friendly but sometimes tricky skies of the Caribbean:

- Always have a reservation.
- Reconfirm 72 hours before departure.
- Get to the airport at least an hour before departure—overbooking can be a problem.
- Never fly standby, especially during peak periods—you won't get on.
- Go immediately to the gate once you've checked in. We were left behind once when the plane arrived early and took off early without us.
- Avoid itinerary changes when flying on Sunday. Everything, including reservation lines and ticket counters, closes down on some islands.
- Keep luggage to a minimum. Carrying a lot in the heat is unpleasant.
- Carry all valuables with you—don't check them! Guard your passport with your life (especially if you're connecting in Miami—we had one stolen there)! A U.S. passport is worth thousands of dollars on the black market.

The main regional airlines, their hubs, and contact info are as follows:

Air Caraïbes (Guadeloupe and Martinique): 877-772-1005, www.aircaraibes.com

Air Jamaica (Montego Bay and Kingston): 800-523-5585, www.airjamaica.com

Caribbean Airlines (Trinidad): 800-920-4225, www.caribbean-airlines.com. Note that Caribbean Airlines has replaced all operations that were once held by the former BWIA.

Caribbean Star and **Caribbean Sun Airlines** (Antigua and San Juan): 866-864-6272, www.flycaribbeanstar.com, www.flycsa.com

Dutch Antilles Express (Bonaire): 011-599-717-0808, www.flydae .com.

LIAT (Antigua): 866-549-5428 or 268-462-0700, www.liatairline .com

Mustique Airways (St. Vincent): 800-526-4789 or 784-458-4380, www.mustiqueairways.com

SVG Air (St. Vincent): 784-457-5124, www.svgair.com

Trans Island Air (TIA) (St. Vincent): 246-418-1654, www.tia2000 .com

Winair (St. Maarten): 011-599-545-4237, www.fly-winair.com

Although Air Jamaica and Caribbean Airlines fly both jets and smaller planes, the other island airlines all fly small planes, from the 19-seat DeHavilland Twin Otter to the 44-seat Dash 8.

Other Airfare Tips

Be sure to check the Internet; deals are always available there. Always shop around and ask for the lowest fare, not just a discount fare. If you're adventurous, call again as your departure date draws nearer — additional low-cost seats may have become available. You can also investigate the major travel tour companies for a charter flight.

Island-Activities Matchup

In *Rum & Reggae's Caribbean*, we include this chart for those in search of the best island for diving, golf, restaurants, gay nightlife, or whatever else is needed to satisfy their Caribbean vacation desires. We've decided to leave the entire chart in this edition of *Rum & Reggae's Puerto Rico, Including Culebra & Vieques* so that readers can see that these three islands (in boldface) appear in many categories.

BEACHES

Anegada
Anguilla
Antigua
Barbuda
Culebra
Dominican Republic
Los Roques
St. Barth
St. John

PRIVACY

Anguilla
The Grenadines
Nevis
Vieques

SCUBA

Bonaire
Cayman Islands
Dominica
Saba

SNORKELING

British Virgin Islands
Culebra
St. John

HEDONISM & NIGHTLIFE

Barbados
Cuba (Havana)
Dominican Republic
    (Santo Domingo)
Jamaica (Negril)
Puerto Rico (San Juan)
St. Martin/St. Maarten
Trinidad (during Carnival)

GAY NIGHTLIFE

Dominican Republic
    (Santo Domingo)
Puerto Rico (San Juan)

SAILING

Antiqua
British Virgin Islands
The Grenadines

CULTURE

Cuba
Curaçao
Jamaica
Martinique
Trinidad

COOKIE-CUTTER
MEGA-RESORTS

Aruba
Grand Cayman
Dominican Republic
Jamaica
Puerto Rico
St. Thomas

FOOD

Anguilla
Guadeloupe
Martinique
Puerto Rico
St. Barth
St. Martin.
St. Thomas

GOLF

Barbados
Dominican Republic
Jamaica
Puerto Rico

NATURE
- Bonaire
- Dominica
- Guadeloupe
- Martinique
- Saba
- St. John
- Trinidad and Tobago

QUIET
- Anguilla
- Bonaire
- **Culebra**
- The Grenadines
- Montserrat
- Nevis
- Saba
- St. Eustatius
- Tobago
- **Vieques**

WINDSURFING
- Aruba
- Barbados
- Bonaire
- Dominican Republic (Cabarete)

- Guadeloupe
- **Puerto Rico (Rincón)**

LUXURY
- Anguilla
- Barbados
- The British Virgin Islands
- The Grenadines (Canouan, Mustique, Petit St. Vincent)
- Nevis
- St. Barth

NUDE BEACHES
- Bonaire
- Guadeloupe
- Jamaica
- St. Martin

SUN
- Anegada
- Anguilla
- Aruba
- Barbuda
- Bonaire
- Curaçao
- Los Roques
- Margarita

Puerto Rico, Culebra, and Vieques Superlatives

Best Beach — Playa Flamenco, Culebra

Best New Destination — Isabela

Best Large Luxury Resort (over 100 rooms) — Rincón of the Seas — Grand Caribbean Hotel, Rincón

Best Small Luxury Resort (under 100 rooms) — Horned Dorset Primavera, Rincón

Best Resort for Kids — El San Juan Hotel & Casino, Isla Verde

Best Romantic Hotel — Casa Flamboyant, Naguabo

Best Boutique Hotel — San Juan Water & Beach Club, Isla Verde

Sexiest Hotel — Bravo Beach Hotel, Vieques

Best Large Hotel — San Juan Marriott Resort & Stellaris Casino, Condado

Best Small Hotel — Numero Uno, Ocean Park

Best City Hideout Hotel — At Wind Chimes Inn, Condado

Best Inn — Hacienda Tamarindo, Vieques

Best Beach House Accommodation — Casa Isleña, Rincón

Best Eco-Friendly "Green" Hotel — La Finca Caribe, Vieques

Best Gay-Friendly Accommodation — Inn on the Blue Horizon, Vieques

Best Room with a View — The Gallery Inn, Old San Juan

Best Fusion Restaurant — Pikayo, Santurce

Best Caribbean-Style Restaurant — Pamela's, Ocean Park

Best Nuevo Latino Restaurant — The Parrot Club, Old San Juan

Best Puerto Rican Restaurant — Ajili Mójili, Old San Juan

Best French Restaurant — Horned Dorset Primavera, Rincón

Best Pan-Asian Restaurant — Dragonfly, Old San Juan

Best Sushi — Sake, Old San Juan

Best Italian Restaurant — Il Perugino, Old San Juan

Best Romantic Seaside Restaurant — Eclipse, Villa Montaña Resort, Isabela

Best Steak House — Ruth's Chris, Isla Verde

Best Café con Leche — Kasalta Bakery, Ocean Park

Best Lunch Spot — Hostería del Mar, Ocean Park

Best Beachside Party Spot — Tamboo, Rincón

Best Piña Colada — The Terrace Bar, Caribe Hilton

Best Place for a Sunset Cocktail — Horned Dorset Primavera, Rincón

Best Place for Nightlife — San Juan

Best Place for Live Music—Nuyorican Café, San Juan

Best Nightclub—Luxor (formerly called Stargate), San Juan

Best Gay Nightclub—Krash Klub (formerly Eros), San Juan

Best Drink with a View—Wet (in the San Juan Water & Beach Club Hotel), San Juan

Best Best Place for Gay Nightlife—San Juan

Best Diving—Culebra

Best Historical Site—Castillo de San Felipe del Morro, Old San Juan

Best Snorkeling—Culebrita

Best Camping—Playa Flamenco, Culebra

Best Golf—Dorado

Best Hike—El Yunque

Best Tennis—Wyndham Río Mar Beach Resort & Spa, Río Mar

Best Windsurfing—Rincón

Best Shopping—Old San Juan

Best T-Shirt—Mamacita's, Culebra

Best Bargain—the guesthouses of Ocean Park

Best-Kept Secret—Culebra

The 10 Best Beaches in Puerto Rico, Culebra, and Vieques (in alphabetical order)

Boquerón, PR

This is a beautiful crescent of golden sand on a tranquil bay. It's best on weekdays.

Crash Boat, Aguadilla, PR

In addition to serving as a landing for Puerto Rico's unique and striking crash boats (some of which grace the cover of this book), this beach is a great place for swimming, snorkeling, or surfing.

Guánica Forest Reserve, PR

This reserve offers lots of small, private beach coves facing an island of picturesque palms.

Luquillo, PR

Luquillo is one of the prettiest beaches on the north coast, and it's still lovely despite encroaching development. Trade winds keep it cool, too.

Navio Beach, Vieques

Navio is an ideal place for peace and quiet. We still can't get over how blue the water is here.

Ocean Park, Santurce, PR

Most visitors agree that this is one of the best city beaches in the region. The sand is powdery and the breezes steady.

Playa Flamenco, Culebra

This is an almost perfect crescent of blindingly white sand, often with body-surfable waves in the wintertime.

Playa Succia, Cabo Rojo, PR

Located just east of Faro de Cabo Rojo, this beach remains a reasonably well-kept secret.

Playa Zoni, Culebra

Always empty, this white-sand beach faces a tranquil bay and Culebrita.

Sun Bay, Vieques

We like this long crescent because it's big, it's close to town, and it has facilities.

Rum & Reggae's Caribbean Cocktails

Rum & Reggae's Punch

Are you dreaming about the tropics, but it's snowing outside? Don't worry, you can create your own Caribbean vision with this recipe.

Ingredients

1 lime
4 oz. water
2–3 oz. good dark rum (the stronger, the better)
2 oz. sugar syrup*
bitters
ice
freshly grated nutmeg

Directions

Squeeze the lime and add the juice and water to the rum and sugar syrup in a tall glass. Shake bitters into the glass four times. Add the rocks, then sprinkle with freshly grated nutmeg (it must be fresh!). Yum! Serves one.

* To make sugar syrup, combine 1 lb. of sugar and 2 cups of water in a saucepan. Boil for about two minutes for sugar to dissolve. Let cool. Keep handy for quick and easy rum punches.

Rum & Reggae's Piña Colada

Ingredients

1 oz. Coco López (or any coconut cream)
1 oz. heavy cream (yes, this is a fattening drink!)
2 oz. light rum (preferably Bacardi or Don Q)
2 oz. unsweetened pineapple juice (fresh is best)

Directions

Mix with 2/3 cup crushed ice in blender until creamy smooth.

Garnish with a slice of fresh pineapple and a cherry (the latter just for the visual). Enjoy!

Puerto Rico

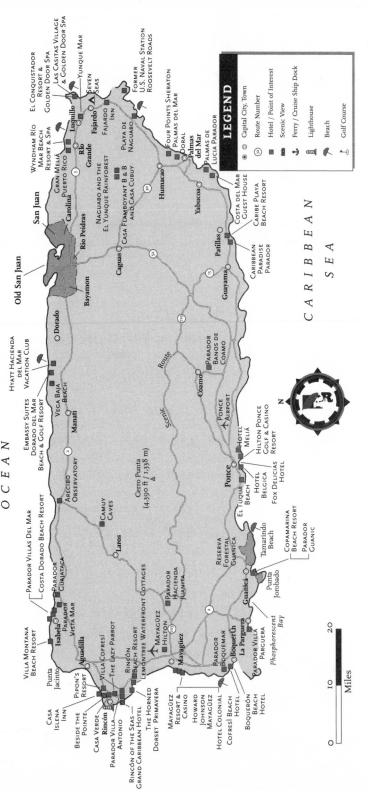

ATLANTIC OCEAN

CARIBBEAN SEA

C A R I B B E A N   S E A

LEGEND

◉	Capital City, Town
🔟	Route Number
■	Hotel / Point of Interest
📷	Scenic View
⚓	Ferry / Cruise Ship Dock
🗼	Lighthouse
🏖	Beach
⛳	Golf Course

San Juan

Old San Juan

El Conquistador Resort & Golden Door Spa

Las Casitas Village & Golden Door Spa

Yunque Mar

Seven Seas

Former U.S. Naval Station Roosevelt Roads

Wyndham Río Mar Beach Resort & Spa

Luquillo

Fajardo Inn

Fajardo

Río Grande

Gran Meliá Puerto Rico

Carolina

Naguabo and the El Yunque Rainforest

Playa de Naguabo

Four Points Sheraton Palmas del Mar

Doral

Palmas del Mar

Palmas de Lucía Parador

Río Piedras

Casa Flamboyant B & B and Casa Cubuy

Humacao

Yabucoa

Costa del Mar Guest House

Caribe Playa Beach Resort

Bayamón

Caguas

Patillas

Caribbean Paradise Parador

Guayama

Dorado

Hyatt Hacienda del Mar Vacation Club

Embassy Suites Dorado del Mar Beach & Golf Resort

Vega Baja Beach

Manatí

Parador Baños de Coamo

Coamo

Arecibo Observatory

Cerro Punta (4,390 ft / 1,338 m)

Camuy Caves

Ponce Airport

Hotel Meliá

Hilton Ponce Golf & Casino Resort

Hotel Belgica

Fox Delicias Hotel

Ponce

El Tuque Beach

Parador Villas Del Mar

Costa Dorado Beach Resort

Parador Guajataca

Parador Vistá Mar

Villa Montana Beach Resort

Punta Jacinto

Isabela

Aguadilla

Larós

Villa Cofresí

The Lazy Parrot

Rincón Beach Resort

Lemontree Waterfront Cottages

Parador Hacienda Juanita

Mayagüez

Hilton

Reserva Forestal Guánica

Copamarina Beach Resort

Parador Guánic

Tamarindo Beach

Guánica

Punta Jorobado

Phosphorescent Bay

Casa Isleña Inn

Beside the Pointe

Casa Verde

Rincón

Parador Villa Antonio

Rincón of the Seas Grand Caribbean Hotel

The Horned Dorset Primavera

Pipón's Resort

Mayagüez Resort & Casino

Howard Johnson Mayagüez

Hotel Colonial

Cofresí Beach Hotel

Boquerón Beach Hotel

Parador Boquemar

Boquerón

La Parguera

Parador Villa Parguera

Route Scenic

N

P R

0		
	10	
		20
	Miles	

Puerto Rico

TOURISTO SCALE:
ﮩﮩﮩﮩﮩﮩﮩﮩﮩ (9)

The first time, we were surprised by it. The next time, we were amused by it. By now, we have come to expect it. Just as the jet's wheels scrape the runway at San Juan's Luis Muñoz Marín International Airport, there is almost always a burst of applause. For the most part, the applause does not come from the tourists, but from the Puerto Ricans. Their trip has ended safely and they are happy to be home. This ritual always causes us to chuckle; it's so genuine that even our jaded cynicism melts away. And hell, we're also pleased to be here 'cuz we just *love* Puerto Rico. Why? Well, not just because this is a beautiful and diverse island, but because of the people. Puerto Ricans, also called Boricuas (the Taíno or Indian name), are very happy, warm people who appear to always be up and ready for a good time. *Party* seems to be their collective middle name.

Puerto Rico is a big island, roughly the size of Connecticut. It is home to more than 3.9 million people, a major metropolis with a diverse economy, mountains, a rainforest, miles of beautiful beaches, the hip swaying beat of salsa, and the "She Bangs" hip thrusts of Ricky Martin. Because Puerto Rico is a commonwealth of the United States, the American influence is very pervasive—from every conceivable

Puerto Rico: Key Facts

Location	18°N by 65°W 70 miles east of the Dominican Republic 1,040 miles southeast of Miami 1,662 miles southeast of New York
Size	3,423 square miles 110 miles long by 35 miles wide
Highest point	Cerro de Punta (4,390 feet)
Population	3.95 million
Language	Spanish; English is officially the second language and is widely spoken in San Juan.
Time	Atlantic Standard Time (1 hour ahead of EST, same as EDT)
Area code	787 (must be dialed before all local numbers as well)
Electricity	110 volts AC, same as U.S. and Canada
Currency	The U.S. dollar
Driving	On the right
Documents	None for Americans and no Customs hassles, either. Canadians need a passport if traveling by air, or proof of nationality (birth certificate, certificate of citizenship, and government-issued photo ID) if arriving by sea. By January 2008, Canadians will need a passport even if traveling by sea. Brits need a visa unless they hold an e-passport or a passport conforming to certain other specific U.S. government requirements. (Check with the U.S. Consulate or your travel agent for more specifics.)
Departure tax	None
Beer to drink	Medalla
Rum to drink	Don Q or Bacardi
Music to hear	Salsa or *reggaetón*!
Tourism info	787-721-2400, 800-866-7827, or 800-223-6530, www.gotopuertorico.com, www.prtourism.com, or www.puertoricowow.com

fast-food and convenience chain (there are more than 50 Burger Kings on the island) to the huge pharmaceutical and high-tech companies. This is unfortunate but inevitable. The culture is still Latino and the language is still Spanish, but most Puerto Ricans speak English or at least understand it to a degree. Former Governor Pedro Roselló reinstated the policy that Puerto Rico has two official languages — Spanish and English — to encourage bilingualism among the populace and inch the island toward statehood. More often than not, however, you'll hear and marvel at the hybrid, commonly known as Spanglish.

Most visitors who come to Puerto Rico see only San Juan (or its airport). San Juan is a city of about 450,000 residents, or Sanjuaneros, as the locals are called. There are more than 1.3 million inhabitants, when you include the surrounding metropolitan area. San Juan is where most of the big hotels and casinos are located. It is also the second largest cruise-ship port after Miami. The combination ensures lots of tourists, especially in places like Old San Juan and Isla Verde. But San Juan is a big city, and with it comes the best nightlife (both straight and gay) in the Caribbean. If you want great restaurants, big and lively casinos (without the Las Vegas tackiness), pulsating nightclubs, and some of the hottest men and women you'll ever mix with — look no farther for your next vacation spot. If you're single, you're crazy not to go here.

There is much more to Puerto Rico than the throbbing beat of San Juan, however. There are beautiful mountains and lush valleys, and small seaside towns with lots of character, like Boquerón and Guánica. There is Puerto Rico's second city, Ponce, which has undergone a restoration similar to Old San Juan. There is some of the best golf in the Caribbean at the Dorado Beach area. There are the extraordinary Camuy Caves — huge natural caverns several hundred feet in the earth. There is great windsurfing off Rincón on the west coast. There are the unspoiled out-islands of Culebra and Vieques (detailed in their own chapters). There is the Caribbean National Forest, El Yunque, which is an easily accessed rainforest. There are deserted beaches on all sides of the island. Even so, you're never more than a two-hour drive from San Juan or very far from an ATM and a Big Gulp from 7-Eleven.

Puerto Rico gets all kinds of tourists and travelers. There are the convention and tour groups who come for a purpose as well as to play in the big casinos and on the beach. There is that element of middle America that always seems to find its way here via the cruise ships that flood Old San Juan. There are lots of European tourists, especially Germans, and rich South Americans up on shopping sprees. Of course, most of the visitors here are American. Then there are the independent travelers who dive into the culture and countryside in search of the real Puerto Rico, and the long-weekenders down for a dose of sun and fun because San Juan is so easy (and cheap) to reach.

The Briefest History

Puerto Rico was first settled by Taíno Amerindians who ventured up the chain of the West Indies from the Amazon and South America. They had been on the island for thousands of years when Columbus landed here on his second voyage, in 1493. He discovered about 60,000 Taíno Amerindians, living off the land and sea, who had named the island Boriquen. Spain claimed the island, and Columbus called it San Juan. With Columbus was Juan Ponce de León, Mr. Fountain of Youth himself, who sensed gold in "them-thar hills" and received permission to colonize the island. It was Ponce de León who, in 1508, renamed this "rich port" Puerto Rico upon becoming governor of its first Spanish settlement at Caparra. That site became disease-ridden, so in 1521 the settlement was moved to what is now Old San Juan. It became a fortress with El Morro fort at its entrance.

The Spanish never lost control of Puerto Rico for more than 400 years, despite repeated attempts by the British, French, and Dutch to dislodge them. It wasn't until the Spanish-American War in 1898, when Teddy Roosevelt led the charge up that hill in Havana shouting "Remember the Maine" and defeated the Spanish, that control ceded to another power: the United States. In 1917 Puerto Ricans became full-fledged U.S. citizens, and in 1952 Puerto Rico became a commonwealth of the United States.

It remains so today. There is an ongoing drive for statehood, which is being spearheaded by the current governor. The most recent plebiscite was to keep the status quo. Under commonwealth status,

Puerto Ricans have a U.S. passport and can live anywhere in the United States. They have local representation in a commonwealth government and pay no federal income tax as residents of Puerto Rico (however, they do pay Puerto Rican government income taxes). The drawback to commonwealth status is that Puerto Ricans have no representation in Congress (nor can they vote for president). However, they do have a nonvoting Interests Section in Congress. No federal taxes and no sales tax—what a deal. We're moving to Puerto Rico!

Getting There

Of all the Caribbean islands, Puerto Rico is the easiest to reach. San Juan has a huge international airport (Luis Muñoz Marín), which is the hub of American Airlines' Caribbean operation, has more than 30 airlines serving it, and receives more than 400 nonstops weekly from the United States. Most major eastern and southern cities have nonstop service to San Juan on American, Jet Blue, Continental, Delta, Northwest, United, US Airways, and American Trans Air. From Canada, connections can be made on several U.S. carriers from Montreal and Toronto; there is service on Canadian Airlines. From Europe, British Airways, Ibéria, and Air France all have nonstop service. American Eagle and LIAT fly to neighboring islands. For the latest information on all the airlines that serve Puerto Rico, check out the Puerto Rico Tourism Company Web site: www.gotopuertorico.com.

Getting Around

With just about every major rental-car player here offering great weekly (and daily) rates, and with so much to see, it makes perfect sense to rent a car. Avis (800-331-1084 or 787-253-5963), Budget (800-527-0700 or 787-791-2311), Hertz (800-654-3131), National (800-227-3876), and Thrifty (253-2680) are all here. We found the best rates with Thrifty—plus, for those headed to Vieques or Culebra, Thrifty is the only major company with a drop-off office in Fajardo. In addition, several local companies might offer you a better rate; try Charlie Car Rental (787-728-2418) and L&M Car Rental (800-666-0807 or 787-791-1160). Check with your credit card company to see what your coverage includes before you rent.

To help plan your travel around the island, there is a newly expanded tourist information center at the airport. Also, the Puerto Rican Tourism Company (PRTC) has instituted a welcome and easy-to-use taxi system at the airport and in the major tourist areas. Outside the baggage claim, there is a taxi stand with several representatives of the PRTC (they wear the "Puerto Rico Does It Better" buttons as well as IDs). The cabs are painted white, with "Taxi Touristicos" and the official logo on the front doors. Fixed rates apply to the major tourist zones. Longer trips are metered. A cab ride from the airport to Isla Verde is $10, to the Condado area is $14, and to Old San Juan is $16 (not including tip).

Within San Juan, there is a good bus system run by the Metropolitan Bus Authority, 787-250-6064. The buses (called *guaguas*) pick up passengers at upright yellow post stops (called *paradas*), and the fare is 25¢ or 50¢.

Públicos (public cars) are cars or minivans that provide low-cost transportation to the main towns in Puerto Rico. Their rates are set by the Public Service Commission. For information call 787-756-1919.

Some words about driving in Puerto Rico: Puerto Rican drivers are pretty crazy behind the wheel, so be alert. On the freeways (called *autopistas*), particularly Route 52 from San Juan to Ponce, the left lane is often much smoother because trucks don't drive on it. Actually, the left lane often seems to be the de facto travel lane, and the right lane the passing lane. However, cars pass on both left and right, depending on what is open. In addition, don't be confused when you see highway mileage signs in kilometers and speed signs in miles. Finally, Puerto Rico is the land of more than a million cars — too many for the current infrastructure. It often seems that everyone who owns a car here is on the road at the same time, especially in the cities. Due to the effects of traffic lights on multilane roads, there are often traffic jams on secondary roads. East of San Juan, on Route 3, traffic can be heavy all the way to Fajardo. Traffic on roads around Ponce (Routes 1 and 2) can also jam up, although a bypass road has alleviated that problem a bit. Of course, all major roads in and around San Juan will be very busy during rush hours, so plan accordingly. Be sure to ask your rental car company for road sign translations (most are in Spanish).

Focus on Puerto Rico:
San Juan—The Long-Weekend Destination

Where to go for a long or extended weekend in the sun? South Beach, in Miami? Forget it! That place is so 15 years ago. The rest of Florida? Nah, it's just not very exotic or exciting. Havana is not yet easily accessible and is technically off-limits to Americans; a quick jaunt there is neither easy nor convenient. Where, then, does one go for a quick tropical getaway? Well, we think it's a no-brainer. There aren't many other choices where the weather is guaranteed hot, the destination is easy to reach for weekends or longer, and there are great choices of restaurants and nightlife. Now the in-the-know are heading to San Juan.

What used to be San Juan's glittering and main tourist destination—the **Condado** area—is still a tad seedy but is showing signs of a comeback. Anchored by the San Juan Marriott (the old Dupont Plaza), the Condado resembles a cross between Waikiki and Miami Beach. There are some art deco buildings, lots of high-rises, many hotel rooms, and a nice beach here. The water is clean and there is surf, so it's fun; and then there are the restaurants and nightlife. **Old San Juan**, home of some of the Caribbean's most valuable Spanish colonial architecture, has also experienced a boom, primarily due to the thriving cruise-ship industry. Though not directly on the beach (but on a rocky point at the entrance to the harbor), this pretty part of the city has some very cool places to stay. There is **Ocean Park**, east of the Condado, with the city's best beach and a string of charming and cheap guesthouses. At the eastern end of the city and very near the airport is **Isla Verde**, where most of San Juan's big and luxury properties are located.

San Juan is reasonably priced (especially with package deals) and now on par with South Beach (the latter's prices have escalated dramatically in the last few years). Although you can go to Miami and taste its nightlife, restaurants, and beaches, here you get all that *and* you're in the tropics. You won't experience a chilling winter cold front in Puerto Rico. The weather is pretty much the same year-round (as in Florida, the summer has more rain), and the summer in San Juan is actually much cooler than in Florida because of the trade winds. Another bonus is that you can drive an hour out of San Juan and be in the mountains, or two hours and be in a beautiful Caribbean beach town. In Miami, where do you go for diversion—Ocala? Finally, Puerto Rico is 100 percent Latin, not semi-Latin like Miami.

Besides nightlife and beaches, San Juan also has lots of historical sites to see, almost all of them in Old San Juan. You could easily spend at least a half day exploring or just hanging out in this beautifully restored part of the city. Our favorite site here is the ✪Castillo de San Felipe del Morro, 501 Calle Norzagaray, 787-729-6754, which is one of the best-preserved Spanish forts in the New World. Located at the mouth of the bay, this six-level fort was the main line of defense for the Spanish. It's open from 9 a.m. until 5 p.m.

Not to be missed are Fuerte San Felipe del Morro (El Morro), Calle del Morro, 787-729-6960, open daily from 9 a.m. to 5 p.m., English tours at 10 a.m. and 3 p.m., admission $3, children under 12 admitted free; Casa Blanca, 787-724-4102, open from 9 a.m. to noon and from 1 to 4:30 p.m., closed Monday, admission $2 for adults, $1 for seniors; Catedral de San Juan, 787-722-0861, open daily from 8 a.m. to 4 p.m. (it houses the remains of Ponce de León); Iglesia San José, 787-725-7501, open daily from 8:30 a.m. to 4 p.m. and for Sunday Mass at noon; Museo Pablo Casals, 787-723-9185, open Tuesday through Saturday from 9:30 a.m. to 5:30 p.m., admission $1; Museo de Arte e Historia de San Juan, 787-724-1875, open Tuesday through Sunday from 10. a.m. to 4 p.m., free admission; Plaza de Armas (the main square of Old San Juan, where San Juan's city hall has been located since 1789); and La Forteleza (which has been the governor's mansion since 1540), 787-721-7000, open Monday through Friday (except holidays) from 9 a.m. to 4 p.m., with tours in English on the hour.

There's a lot more to see—the above are just highlights. Stop in at La Casita, 787-722-1709, open Saturday through Wednesday from 9 a.m. to 8 p.m., and Thursday and Friday until 5:30 p.m. Located on the Plaza de la Dársena by the cruise-ship docks, it's operated by the Puerto Rican Tourism Company and has a wealth of information, walking tours, and maps available.

SAN JUAN

Where to Stay

¡Caramba! There are so many hotels, inns, resorts, guesthouses, and *paradores* in Puerto Rico that the choices are staggering. At last count, Puerto Rico had about 16,000 hotel rooms, with a goal of 19,000 by 2008. Some heavy hitters are expected to arrive in the near future, such as a five-star St. Regis (the Bahía Beach Resort & Golf Club) that could open as early as 2008. W Hotels is planning to assume management of the historic Normandie Hotel in late 2007, and the 500-room Sheraton Puerto Rico Convention Center Hotel should be completed by September 2009.

There are four different parts of San Juan in which you can stay. The primary area is Isla Verde, a newer big-hotel strip near the airport. This is where most of the large hotels are located. We do not recommend staying in Isla Verde if the roar of jets landing and taking off will bother you (it is especially loud once you're east of El San Juan Hotel). Another major area is the more centrally located Condado, once the primary place for hotels and experiencing a renaissance of sorts. Between the Condado and Isla Verde is Ocean Park. This is one of our personal favorites; it's a residential neighborhood of charming two-story homes and some big old stucco houses on the beach. The beach itself is the best in the city (and a pretty beach in its own right). The accommodations here are ✪guesthouses, which are casual, relaxed, beachy, and cheap. We like this combination. The last area is Old San Juan, which is full of colonial architecture and character, although it is inconvenient to the beach, and during the day the cruise ship–tourbus circuit swarms the area. Still, it's unique, and two of the places we recommend there, El Convento and the Gallery Inn, are superb.

Most of the accommodations are right here in San Juan, but, as you'll learn throughout the book, there are certainly great alternatives, like Rincón, Guánica, and Boquerón.

To aid travelers in handling the daunting task of finding hotels in Puerto Rico, the Puerto Rico Tourism Company (PRTC) has recently launched an online reservation system providing info on all

Old San Juan

San Juan

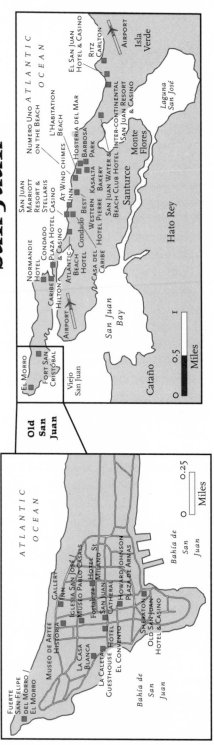

accommodations throughout the island. The Web site allows visitors to perform real-time searches, bookings, and even cancellations. The site includes detailed information on not only the big resorts and hotels but also on many of Puerto Rico's unique *paradores puertorriqueños*—a group of small hotels and inns scattered about the island, often in great locations. Don't expect cute little Vermont-style B&Bs or inns. The *paradores* are generally simple, motelish accommodations that are usually under $100 a night and clean. Some are in the mountains, some are on or near a beach, but they all provide an inexpensive and comfy place to hang your hat while you explore the island. All have basic amenities, like air-conditioning, TV, and phones, and many have pools. To take advantage of the PRTC's comprehensive online system, visit www.gotopuertorico.com or call 800-866-7827 or 787-721-2400 (in San Juan).

With all of this in mind, we did quite a bit of weeding and sifting, which, of course, is our job. Here are our suggestions.

Condado

⊛ **San Juan Marriott Resort & Stellaris Casino**, 1309 Avenida Ashford, San Juan, PR. ✆ 800-464-5005 or 787-722-7000, ✉ 787-289-6082 or 722-6800, 🖳 www.marriott.com

💲 **Ridiculous** and up ⑪ **EP** ⒸⒸ 511 rooms and 14 suites

For years, this has been our favorite place to stay in the Condado, and now that the Marriott has poured another $35 million into a massive renovation project (finally completed in spring 2007), this hotel is leagues above the competition. All 402 rooms in the tower wing have been redecorated in a contemporary Caribbean style, with new plumbing, plasma HDTVs, and plush bedding. The casino, restaurants, meeting rooms, ballroom, and lobby have been revamped as well, and sparkle with glamour. As a matter of fact, we now prefer the Marriott to all the big hotels in San Juan. Its location is perfect, the beach in front is wide and spacious, the pool area is comfortable and private, the staff is friendly and helpful, and the lobby bar is a magnet for good musical talent and Sanjuaneros out for a dressy good time. Best of all, the size of the hotel doesn't overwhelm, and travel time from pool to room is less than five minutes — a major convenience. We also appreciate the fact that the Marriott was key in the renaissance of this part of the Condado, renovating the old Dupont Plaza (closed in 1987 after a tragic fire), putting millions into the 21-story building and compact grounds, and reopening in 1995.

Now that all the rooms have been upgraded, they are even more comfortable than before and include details like Revive bedding, two-line speaker phones, data ports, voicemail, high-speed wireless Internet access, individual climate control, and in-room pay movies on those great HDTVs. The baths are a tad small, but they are clean and modern. All rooms have a lanai. If you get an oceanfront room, the sound of the surf will fill your room, even up to the 20th floor. We like the 24-hour room service, too. After a night on the town, we need something to absorb the alcohol.

Because the Marriott is centrally located, you can walk almost everywhere (except Old San Juan). Even the best nightclubs are an easy walk or cab ride (recommended) away. The resort has a spa, an excellent small gym, two lighted tennis courts, and the Stellaris Casino (which is fortunately located to the side of the lobby and thus not too intrusive). There are a few restaurants here as well, the best being the Italian Tuscany. Late-night diners (and hungry gamblers) will enjoy the Wan Chai Noodle Bar inside the casino. Look for corporate rates and package deals — they can reduce the rates by 30 percent or more.

Note that in the fall of 2007, the Marriott will be undergoing a major renovation of the 123 rooms in the cabana wing. The hotel plans to remain fully operational during this time and expects that the construction should not present much of an inconvenience. (We recommend playing it safe and staying in the tower wing until the project is complete.)

⊛ **At Wind Chimes Inn,** 1750 Avenida McLeary, Condado, San Juan, PR. ℂ 800-946-3244 or 787-727-4153, ✎ 787-728-0671, ⌨ www.atwindchimesinn.com, reservations@atwindchimesinn.com

🔳   **Not So Cheap** ⑪ BP ⒸⒸ 22 rooms

This quaint inn, set in a charming well-preserved Spanish villa that dates back to the Roaring '20s, is the perfect place for anyone seeking solace from the row of high-rise hotels here in the Condado. Just walking through the white arch that separates this tranquil inn from the busy San Juan streets, we felt right at home. Although we have never had a home like this, the phrase seems to work here, as a laid-back air pervades. After all, how hectic can life be in a place named after its wind chimes? The old house retains its colonial feel, embellished by the colorful artwork of the owner's mother, along with period pieces throughout. The different wings have ceramic tile sundecks and Spanish-style patios shaded by bougainvillea and palm trees. Although the inn has been open for more than 20 years, recent improvements have lifted the Wind Chimes to a new level of comfort. The quaint pool, replete with Jacuzzi-bay, provides the perfect cool-off spot for sun lovers. The brand-new tiki boat bar is a great place to check out the murals, enjoy a tropical drink, and dream of the open seas. Also, being just a block from the beach, guests are within range of the Condado's fine sands. The rooms are tastefully decorated with vibrant colors, terra-cotta floors, cable TV, a/c, and a fan. The junior suites, which include balconies and kitchenettes, are especially comfortable. After our enjoyable stay in this picturesque inn, we realized that the Wind Chimes is San Juan's ideal urban oasis.

Caribe Hilton, P.O. Box 9021872, Calle Los Rosales, San Gerónimo Grounds, San Juan, PR. ⓒ 877-GO-HILTON or 787-721-0303, ✎ 787-725-8849, ▢ www.hiltoncaribbean.com/sanjuan

  🛍 **Wicked Pricey** and up ⑪ **EP** CC 812 rooms, suites, and villas

Opened in 1949, the Caribe Hilton is an institution on the island and a focal point of activity in the city. Business, government, and cultural meetings and events happen here regularly. The hotel was extensively renovated in 1999, with a total redesign of the lobby and public areas, a new swimming complex, and a huge health club. Sitting in the breezy lobby of the hotel, you will see people from all walks of life and from everywhere—always a hubbub of activity. The hotel is the biggest in San Juan and a huge property, for being in the midst of a city. Nestled on 17 acres on the other end of the Condado Bridge in an area called Puerto de Tierra, it consists of two multistory buildings and a tower (all of which house 644 rooms and suites) as well as the 168 Condado Lagoon Villas that were added in 2005—like we said, it's a big hotel. There are gardens with fish ponds, a new pool area in the center of the airy Terrace Bar (where the ✪piña colada was invented in 1957), and the private beach, which is man-made but still attractive and protected by a lagoon.

On the grounds are three lighted tennis courts and a new health club and spa. The gym is the largest we've seen at a hotel, period. The size of a school gymnasium, it features lots of free weights, machines, treadmills, and a stadium ceiling. The spa with sauna and Jacuzzi costs extra. There is also a small snack bar. Water sports can be arranged by the hotel. The recently redone rooms are a mix of pastel and dark green, with wall-to-wall carpeting and marble baths. Most rooms have lanais and all the amenities you would expect from a major international hotel. The 168 Condado Lagoon Villas are a great option. They feature huge space with studio, one-bedroom, or two-bedroom configurations. Each includes a living room, full kitchen, private terrace, and ocean views. There are nine restaurants, two bars, and a newly renovated casino. We love the fact that the hotel often has great Latino bands at the Oasis Bar, which has always been well attended by dressed-up locals. Also available is the Executive Business Center, which is free for use by hotel guests. For a fee, it will also provide secretarial and translation services, fax and photocopy service, the use of PCs with high-speed Internet, and binding. Check for corporate rates or package deals.

Note that the Caribe Hilton has recently taken over management of the villas at the neighboring Paseo Caribe (a time-ownership property where the individual unit owners are limited to 90 days a year). This, along with the ongoing Paseo Caribe construction project, will push the hotel's room count to well over 900, making it the largest hotel property in Puerto Rico.

Condado Plaza Hotel & Casino, P.O. Box 1270, 999 Avenida Ashford, San Juan, PR. © 866-317-8934 or 787-721-1000, ✆ 787-722-7955, 🖥 www.condadoplaza.com

💲 **Wicked Pricey** 🍴 **EP** ⒸⒸ 570 rooms and 62 suites

The Condado Plaza is another large hotel and is on the other side of the bridge from the Caribe Hilton. Although it doesn't have an impressive lobby, it does have a fairly airy manageable casino with windows, so you know when the sun is coming up and when it's time for bed. The best thing about the hotel is the spacious and fun pool area (there are three declared pools — one is salt water). The hotel is on a small, calm public beach, anchoring one end of the bridge that spans the lagoon. Condado spent $40 million for a much-needed refurbishing in 1998. Also, with LXR Luxury Resorts' recent acquisition of the property, much more money has been poured into renovating the rooms. The rooms are attractive and comfortably furnished, and most have private balconies and all the standard amenities, including 24-hour room service and an iron and ironing board. The hotel consists of two buildings connected by a bridge over the road (we prefer the oceanside one). There are six very different restaurants as well as the Casino Lounge, which has live Latin bands (we like that). The newest restaurant addition is the Strip House, a New York–style steakhouse that opened in 2007. There are two lighted tennis courts, a water sports complex offering kayaks and windsurfing (extra charge), and a fitness center with sauna and steam (extra charge). Look for package deals.

Normandie Hotel, P.O. Box 50059, Avenida Riviera, at the New Millennium Park, San Juan, PR. © 877-987-2929 or 787-729-2929, ✆ 787-729-3083, 🖥 www.normandiepr.com

💲 **Very Pricey** 🍴 **EP** ⒸⒸ 173 rooms

The stylish Normandie was reopened in January 2000 after it had been severely damaged by 1998's Hurricane Georges.

Recently, the hotel completed an $8 million renovation that included 7,000 square feet of meeting space, wireless access throughout the property, a couple of 800-gallon fish tanks that adorn the lobby, two restaurants, a lounge, a state-of-the art fitness center, and the N Spa — an indoor-outdoor full-service spa.

Located next to the Caribe Hilton complex and on a slice of beach, this luxury liner–shaped structure is San Juan's only real art deco hotel. Except for the ship shape, it looks like it's right out of South Beach. The new lobby is on the small side, giving the hotel more of an inn feeling than the boutique appearance that they are looking for. The décor, though warm, isn't carried out throughout the hotel. There is a large atrium inside with the usual glass elevator and a restaurant and the sleek N Bar. But the place screams for a decorator and some foliage. The hotel states that the redecorated rooms feature a "cabin style" (remember, this is supposed to be an art deco "luxury liner"), but they are more a mélange than art deco. We want to warm this place up. The pool, though offering an OK sundeck, is small and in need of better landscaping (you must walk from the hotel across the asphalt driveway to reach it — a missed opportunity).

At press time, the property was still undergoing renovations (which were said to include a new pool area and a signature restaurant) and was slated to be transformed into a W Hotel. Thus, we expect that any of the Normandie's shortcomings will be remedied by this chic and contemporary hotel group.

Best Western Hotel Pierre, 105 Avenida de Diego, Santurce, San Juan, PR. © 800-528-1234 or 787-721-1200, ✆ 787-721-3118, 🖳 www.bestwestern.com

🛨 **Pricey** and up ⑪ **CP** CC 183 rooms

Although it's not anywhere close to the beach (it's a 10-minute walk), the Hotel Pierre is a very attractive property and an excellent value for a full-service hotel in the Condado area. It's very popular with the business set, which is always a good sign. The lobby features marble floors and plenty of places to sit, chat on your cell phone, and plan your day or evening. There's even a small gym with a sauna. The hallways have attractive dropped ceilings of wooden slats, and all the rooms have new bathrooms, refrigerators, and microwave ovens. All rooms have a/c, phones, free Internet access, and cable TV. There are three restaurants, a bar, and a pool on the grounds. Look for packages or corporate rates.

Casa del Caribe, 57 Calle Caribe, Condado, San Juan, PR.
ⓒ 877-722-7139 or 787-722-7139, ✆ 787-728-2575,
🖳 www.casadelcaribe.net, reservations@casadelcaribe.net

💲 **Cheap** 🍴 **CP** ⒸⒸ 13 rooms

The title "tropical bed and breakfast" might be a bit of a stretch—the conditions are far from tropical, and the breakfast is not much to speak of, either, but we cannot deny that this cute inn is a suitable alternative for those who are seeking a cheap stay in the otherwise pricey Condado. We had no problem taking advantage of the fancy bars and beach of the "conveniently located" Marriott, just a block away. Housed in a 70-year-old building on a relatively quiet side street, its rooms are simple but comfortable, equipped with pumping a/c, phone, private (though outdated) bath, and cable TV. Under new management, the Casa del Caribe has a super-friendly staff ready to assist guests in their San Juan endeavors. Parking is available for $5.

Atlantic Beach Hotel, 1 Calle Vendig, Condado, San Juan, PR.
ⓒ 787-721-6900, ✆ 787-721-6917,
🖳 www.atlanticbeachhotel.com,
reservations@atlanticbeachhotel.net

💲 **Not So Cheap** 🍴 **CP** ⒸⒸ 36 rooms

This is the Condado's gay hotel and the site of a daily happy hour (4 to 6 p.m.) that is popular with both tourists and locals. This place needs not only a face-lift but some lipo and major tucking, too. To quote the late great Bette Davis, "What a dump!" If you want to stay in a gay-friendly environment, stay at one of the guesthouses in Ocean Park (see below). The bar, however, is definitely fun for happy hour, especially on Sunday. There is a restaurant adjoining the bar. Given the orientation of the hotel's guests, the beach in front is Condado's gay beach (the hotel provides chaises).

Isla Verde

Isla Verde is a strip of large condos and hotels on the beach side, and every conceivable fast-food joint known to humanity is on the other. The beach here is nice, and some people seem to love staying in this part of San Juan. Our biggest gripe is that the airport is down the street; we loathe the sound of screaming jet engines while we're reading Jane Austen (very incongruous, indeed!). Incredibly, hotel chains keep building here, including the fairly new Ritz-Carlton, which is literally across the street from the end of the runway where the jumbo jets rev their engines to take off. Hello? Anybody home? Fortunately, El San Juan and the Inter-Continental (née The Sands), are far enough away so that the noise is only a dull roar. We also find it rather removed from the nightlife and restaurant scene—a car or significant taxi ride is necessary. But the airport is close!

⊛ **San Juan Water & Beach Club Hotel**, 2 Calle José Tartak, Isla Verde, San Juan, PR. ℂ 888-265-6699 or 787-728-3666, ✺ 787-728-3610, 🖳 www.waterclubsanjuan.com

   💲 **Wicked Pricey** 🍴 **EP** CC 78 rooms

   Voted Puerto Rico's top luxury boutique hotel by the 2006 World Travel Awards, this hot spot, formerly just The Water Club, has *sexy* written all over it. Not literally, of course, but with its chic ambiance and array of sensual restaurants and bars, some couples never make it out the front door. The Water Club debuted in late 2001, and the intent was to create an environment that has more in common with a Manhattan boutique hotel than with a typical beach resort. The recent name change was meant only to clear up confusion that it was a members-only property (which it's not) — the style and vibe remain the same. Although the hotel sits across the street from a good beach, the focus is on the modern, wallpaper-worthy interiors — no generic tropical print bedspreads here.

Falling water is a key element of the concept: There's a waterfall over corrugated metal behind the main bar, glass-enclosed waterfalls tumble inside the elevators (quite a head rush when the elevator zips up and down), and a hall mirror on each floor is drizzled with trickling water. The central lighting scheme throughout is dark and neon blue — votive candles glow in the lobby and hallways 24/7. By day, the rooms are stylish and bright, with blond wood floors (faux, but attractive) and king-size beds angled toward the water; all rooms have at least a partial ocean view. All of the au courant furnishings were designed to order. The recently renovated sexy bathrooms include double-head showers with glass doors and stainless steel pedestal sinks. There are special touches, like the CD and TV stand on a floor-to-ceiling swivel, clock radios with MP3 player connections, in-room Wi-Fi access, and the "desires" board — a glass notepad and pen for guests to make maid requests. There are a few annoyances: The rooms don't have a real closet, just a recess in the wall with a hanger, and, at the prices charged here, isn't collecting a rental fee for the front desk's library of CDs a little much?

There is a tiny yet very chic rooftop pool, where Sunday afternoon champagne parties are staged. Adjoining the pool is a bar, called Wet, which has a terrific view and offers sushi and even has a fireplace. On the ground floor is the restaurant, Tangerine, which is a small dining room decorated in white and orange with smooth curves and sharp lines. Room service is 24 hours, and the food is delicious, if somewhat skimpy in the portion department. The Water Club is located about a half mile west of El San Juan, on a dead-end street that becomes jammed with traffic on Friday and Saturday nights. Yes, San Juan's cogniscetti discovered this spot instantly, and as long as the hotel stays in favor with that crowd, this will be the scene to beat.

⊛ **El San Juan Hotel & Casino**, P.O. Box 9022872, 6063 Avenida
Isla Verde, San Juan, PR. ℭ 866-317-8935 or 787-791-1000,
🕾 787-791-0390, ▢ www.thesanjuanhotel.com

💲 **Wicked Pricey** and up 🍴 **EP** CC 385 rooms, 21 suites

El San Juan is the largest deluxe hotel-resort-casino property
in Isla Verde, located on more than 15 acres. Its entrance —
through a dim carved-mahogany lobby with a massive crystal
chandelier hovering over the bar like the cloud shadow in a
Magritte painting — is impressively different from most tropical hotels. The floors are dark marble. To the right is the best
looking and most spacious casino in San Juan. To the left is
the reception area, and beyond it the pools and beach. The
outside area is fantastic. There are several pools, including a
nice-size lap pool and the requisite resort pool with waterfalls
and islands. Around it are a Jacuzzi and some very comfortable chaises with cushions (which we love). Pool bars seem to
be everywhere, and overall it is a very attractive setting. There
are ocean premier suites (*casitas*), which can be rented, that
border one of the best big-hotel beaches in San Juan. Two
lighted tennis courts and water sports round out the outdoor
activities. The rooms are decorated in shades of yellow and
green and have dark wood colonial-style furnishings. Although the majority of the rooms are on the smallish side,
they are fully loaded with such items as VCR, stereo, a tiny
TV in the bathroom, tile bath, an iron and ironing board, a
hairdryer, and three phones. A new three-story structure on
the grounds houses 21 luxury suites with the same amenities
but with more space and privacy. Although we were impressed with the brand new 409-square foot La Vista and
Grande Vista rooms, they do not offer vistas of the ocean.
Rather, they have views of the San Juan skyline or Avenida
Isla Verde — not bad, but not the ocean. On the roof of the
main building is the Rooftop Spa and Fitness Center with
steam and sauna. Downstairs there are seven dinner restaurants, two snack bars, eight cocktail lounges (including the
Tequila Bar on the 10th floor and a cigar bar), and the Brava
disco (a dressy club where locals take their dates to impress

them). Although it comes with a hefty price, El San Juan is a good family option because it offers many kids' programs and family packages.

Inter-Continental San Juan Resort & Casino, 5961 Avenida Isla Verde, Isla Verde, San Juan, PR (mailing address: P.O. Box 6676, Loíza Station, Santurce, PR 00914-6676). Ⓒ 888-424-6835 or 787-791-6100, ✎ 787-253-2510, ⌨ www.interconti.com, sanjuan@interconti.com

💲 **Wicked Pricey** and up 🍴 **EP** ⒸⒸ 402 rooms

Formerly the San Juan Grand, the Inter-Continental San Juan received a $15 million face-lift when it was the San Juan Grand, and, more recently, its pool and Italian restaurant (soon to become Alfredo Di Roma) were remodeled. It still has that fabulous early '60s look—but now it's yellow instead of white. The lobby's marble floors are more colorful now, and the mirror-and-chrome motif is gone. There is a good-size casino; when we were there, someone was gambling away thousands of dollars at the craps table (and enjoying every minute, strangely enough). Outside, there is a large free-form pool (reportedly the largest free-form pool in the Caribbean with Jacuzzi and swim-up bar) with the standard tropical resort feature of an island in the middle with bridges. There is a spacious beach in front with chaises. The rooms all have little lanais with soundproof sliders. The new décor features modern furnishings, gold-tone carpeting, yellow walls, artwork with dark woodwork, and a distinctly international or European feel. The renovated hallways feature dark mahogany woodwork and gold striated wallpaper. There are also two bars and three well-frequented restaurants on the premises, including Ruth's Chris Steak House (San Juan's best steak house). Look for packages.

The Ritz-Carlton San Juan Hotel & Casino, 6961 Avenida de los Gobernadores, Isla Verde, Carolina, PR. Ⓒ 800-241-3333 or 787-253-1700, ✎ 787-253-1777, ⌨ www.ritzcarlton.com

💲 **Wicked Pricey** and up 🍴 **EP** ⒸⒸ 416 rooms

Although this hotel is a Ritz—down to the crystal chandeliers, oriental rugs, dark heavy furniture (which we found rather out of place in tropical Puerto Rico), afternoon tea, and its renowned service—we couldn't grasp why it would build this resort (opened in 1997) adjacent to the runway of the international airport. The noise, especially on the entrance side, is horrendous when the jumbo jets rev their engines to take off. Even on the ocean side, where the very pretty and well-designed pool area is located, the roar of the jets could be heard through our iPod headphones (we were playing Beyoncé—Joni Mitchell couldn't compete with the planes). The windows of this oversize hotel are double-paned for noise insulation and do not open. Of the hundreds of rooms available, only 21 offer lanais, and they are on the ocean side. Our room was on the airport side, and we heard what sounded like muffled screams every time a plane took off. If this will bother you (as it did us), then look elsewhere.

Otherwise, this is a fine hotel, and it features the largest casino in Puerto Rico. All the amenities that make the Ritz famous are available, including twice-daily maid service and those sumptuous terry-cloth bathrobes. There is 24-hour room service, served with silver and china on a wheeled-in table—wonderful to enjoy while wearing those robes, a Ritz experience. Our standard room was on the smallish side, with dark wall-to-wall carpeting, mahogany furniture, and brightly colored upholstery. The baths are a symphony of marble.

Besides the pool (between jets) and the robes, we loved the Ritz's spa and fitness center, contained in a wing of the hotel. A 12,000-square-foot space, the gym is one of the best of any hotel on the island and includes a fabulous aerobics room with nine spinners, treadmills, and stationary bikes. All kinds of body pampering is available, as well as fitness and aerobics classes. There are two lighted tennis courts, a pretty beach (for a city beach) in front, and all kinds of water sports available through the hotel. There are three restaurants, two bars, and the only casino in the Ritz chain. Check for corporate rates or packages.

Ocean Park

This is a wonderful residential neighborhood without high-rise hotels and with the best beach in San Juan. There are several guesthouses, three of which we recommend. All are mixed gay and straight, with L'Habitation Beach Guest House being the gayest, but everyone of any persuasion is welcome.

(★) **Numero Uno on the Beach**, 1 Calle Santa Ana, Ocean Park, San Juan, PR. (℃) 866-726-5010 or 787-726-5010, ✆ 787-727-5482, 💻 www.numero1guesthouse.com, info@numero1guesthouse.com

($) **Not So Cheap** and up (🍽) **CP** (CC) 11 rooms, 3 suites

Numero Uno is one of our favorite places to stay in Puerto Rico and the best accommodation of its kind in San Juan. Located on the beach, this three-story guesthouse is beautifully relaxed, friendly, and comfortable. Owners Chris and Ester Laube (ex–New Jerseyans—he's American and she's Puerto Rican) know their business well, having completely renovated a dilapidated old house on the beach and built it into a solid business of repeat customers, all in a decade. Like all other guesthouses in Ocean Park, the clientele here is mixed straight and gay, American and European. Numero Uno's restaurant, Pamela's, is one of the best in San Juan.

The rooms are comfortable and clean—all have a/c, ceiling fans, Internet, double or king-size beds, white tile floors, private baths, and no TVs. The downstairs has a plunge pool and lots of shady places where you can sit and sip a cocktail while you reread *Valley of the Dolls*. The beach in front is never crowded and is sort of the gay section of this stretch of sand. Numero Uno provides chaises and beach towels for its guests.

Hostería del Mar, 1 Calle Tapia, Ocean Park, San Juan, PR. (℃) 877-727-3302 or 787-727-3302, ✆ 787-268-0772, 💻 www.hosteriadelmarpr.com, hosteriadelmar@caribe.net

($) **Cheap** and up (🍽) **EP** (CC) 23 rooms

Situated right on the beach, there is a very tranquil air at Hostería del Mar, apparent as you enter through a gate, pass a goldfish pool, and step into a breezy lounge attractively decorated in light woods, rattans, and tropical plants. To your left is one of our favorite places to have lunch in San Juan (see Where to Eat). The restaurant's setting is extraordinary, especially since it's in a city. Sitting inside, you definitely wouldn't know you were in San Juan—the sound of the surf is omnipresent. The rooms are simply but nicely decorated, with terra-cotta tile floors, rattan furnishings, a/c, cable TV, phones, and private baths. Many rooms have lanais and ocean views, and some have kitchenettes. The beach out front is never crowded.

L'Habitation Beach Guest House, 1957 Calle Italia, Ocean Park, San Juan, PR. ✆ 787-727-2499, ✎ 787-727-2599, 🖳 www.habitationbeach.com, info@habitationbeach.com

💲 **Cheap** 🍴 **CP** 🆑 10 rooms

This beachside gay guesthouse sits next door to Numero Uno and is now owned by Marie and Michel Barrabes, so don't be surprised to hear some French in the halls. Known years ago as the Beach House, L'Habitation Beach Guest House is a simple and casual place to stay, with a sand patio and bar in front for guests. Thankfully, the owners have made good on their promise to give this hotel a spiffing up, and everything has been nicely remodeled. The rooms are basic, clean but comfortable, with cable TV and a/c. The price is right, so don't expect too much. All rooms have ceiling fans and private baths but no room phones. The best and most spacious rooms front the beach (ask for Room 8 or 9). Windows are louvered—there is no glass. There are beach chairs outside and there is free parking for guests.

The beach bar serves burgers and sandwiches for lunch. A complimentary continental breakfast is also served at the beach bar. The guesthouse provides chaises for its guests. L'Habitation prefers adults only.

Old San Juan

Old San Juan now has more lodging possibilities, partly due to the cruise-ship impact on this part of the city, but also due to the beautiful Spanish colonial architecture of the oldest part of the city. In the past few years, the restaurant scene and nightlife have improved in Old San Juan, which also boosts its appeal as a place to stay. Two small hotels, the fabulous Convento and the art-filled Gallery Inn, are great choices for those seeking something different. The Sheraton Old San Juan is a larger chain hotel that caters to the cruise-ship industry. Although there is no beach in Old San Juan (the closest one is in the Condado), it is surrounded by water on three sides. Water views abound from rooftops, from between buildings, and from the steep, narrow streets.

Hotel El Convento, 100 Calle Cristo, Old San Juan, PR.
   ℭ 800-468-2779 or 787-723-9020, ✎ 787-721-2877,
   ▱ www.elconvento.com, info@elconvento.com
▮ **Wicked Pricey** and up ⑪ **CP** CC 68 rooms

Probably the finest small hotel in San Juan (it's the only Small Luxury Hotels of the World member property in Puerto Rico), El Convento resides in a 350-year-old building across from the Cathedral of Old San Juan. Occupied for 250 years by Carmelite nuns, the building was abandoned in 1903 due to neglect. Many uses followed until it was finally purchased in 1995 and experienced a much-needed $16 million face-lift, completed in 1997 and fully utilizing the architectural distinctiveness of the building and its stunning multistoried, arched interior courtyard.

We loved the whole ambiance, look, and energy of this place (maybe all that past praying rubbed off on us a little). The courtyard features several restaurants, including El Picoteo Tapas Bar — the best place for drinks in Old San Juan. (Be careful with the olives in your martini. Savoring that final martini treat, we bit down to discover that it wasn't pitted and consequently cracked a crown. Now that was an expensive drink!) The courtyard also has a shopping arcade on the ground level.

The hotel occupies the top four floors of the building (the lobby is located on the third floor). Access is controlled by an elevator passkey. Guests are met by a porter at the front gate and are escorted to the reception desk. The rooms are all different, in both size and décor. Standard rooms are on the small side—an upgrade might be desired. The walls are brightly colored and hand-painted. The furniture is a mélange of restored mahogany antiques and hand-crafted wrought-iron pieces. All rooms have a/c, CD players, TV-VCRs, two-line phones, free high-speed Internet, fridges, irons and ironing boards, and bathrobes. El Convento also has suites, including the spectacular and intriguing Gloria Vanderbuilt Suite, with marble floors, parlor, hand-painted and -stenciled walls, Spanish colonial antiques, high-beamed ceilings painted blue, vintage art, and black marble bath with Jacuzzi—all for $1,200 a day. There is a new fitness center with treadmills and free weights, a small pool, and a Jacuzzi on a terrace with fab views of the Fortaleza, the Cathedral, and the harbor. Look for packages.

⊛ **The Gallery Inn**, 204 Calle Norzagaray, Old San Juan, PR.
   ℂ 787-722-1808, ✎ 787-977-3929,
   ⌨ www.thegalleryinn.com, reservations@thegalleryinn.com
   💲 **Very Pricey** and up ⑪ **CP** CC 22 rooms

Now this is an unusual place. Packed floor to ceiling with the art of Jan D'Esopo (mostly watercolors and sculptures), the Gallery Inn has the ambiance of a small museum. Indeed, the inn's lobby could easily be mistaken for a cramped art gallery (we weren't even sure we were in the right place). However, the lobby leads to an inner courtyard and working studio with a more comfortable sense of space. We were fascinated by the artwork, which made us a tad dizzy after a while from constantly changing focus. Seated with a cocktail, we regained our composure.

Set in a rambling 350-year-old building at the crest of Old San Juan, this inn has become a popular gathering spot for the young, up-and-coming bohemian crowd. The views from the inn's roof terrace, called the Wine Deck, are breathtaking.

Begun in 1984, the inn has grown over time, and the rooms reflect the owners' constant collecting of interesting furnishings and art. Some might complain that the rooms are not kept up so well, which could be a valid point, but the ambiance seems to make up for it. There are many quiet nooks, crannies, patios, and gardens for repose or reading. There's even an air-conditioned music room with a Steinway grand piano for the pianists among us. Several caged birds also live here, as do the owners, Jan D'Esopo and Manuco Gandía. All the suites and rooms, primarily named after children and grandchildren of Jan and Manuco, are scattered throughout the inn. They are individually decorated and include beds with comfortable Tempur-Pedic mattresses. Each has a private bath, central a/c, a phone, and no TV. The staff here is especially warm and helpful, and an honor bar in the lobby makes an afternoon glass of wine a perfect opportunity to chat with the owners, other guests, or just the parrots.

Sheraton Old San Juan Hotel & Casino, 100 Brumbaugh, Old San Juan, PR. ℂ 866-653-7577 or 787-721-5100, ✆ 787-721-1111, ⌨ www.sheratonoldsanjuan.com

💲 **Very Pricey** and up ⑪ **EP** Ⓒ 240 rooms

Opened in 1997 by Wyndham and recently taken over by Sheraton, this nine-story hotel gets most of its business from cruise-ship customers who stay at the beginning or end of their trips. The hotel has a very small lobby that is dominated by the cacophony of slot-machine bells from the adjoining casino. A $7-million rehab by Sheraton has made a difference: In addition to enhancing the casino, it has added La Fogata restaurant, run by renowned Chef Robert Treviño, who has appeared on the Food Network's *Iron Chef.* The rooms are now more comfortable, too, especially with the Sheraton Sweet Sleeper beds. Deluxe rooms face outside and have stucco walls, blond wood furnishings, wall-to-wall carpeting, and earth-tone fabrics, which were a refreshing change from the omnipresent pastels. We found the rooms and windows smallish, but the baths were more than adequate, with good showerheads and Italian tiles. Other amenities include two-line speakerphones with data ports and voicemail, a safe, satellite TV, and an iron and ironing board. We also liked that feather pillows were available, as well as 24-hour room service. The suites have balconies and views of the bay and old city. There is a small rooftop pool with a tile deck and a great view of the harbor. A tiny fitness center is adjacent. Look for packages or corporate rates.

Hotel Milano, 307 Calle Fortaleza, Old San Juan, PR.
✆ 877-729-9050 or 787-729-9050, ✆ 787-722-3379,
🖵 www.hotelmilanopr.com, info@hotelmilanopr.com
💲 **Not So Cheap** 🍴 **CP** **CC** 30 rooms

Willing to trade style for location? The Milano is housed in a restored colonial building right in the heart of San Juan, which means that guests are steps from shops and restaurants, but there is street noise to deal with as a result. Unfortunately, the Milano does not retain any of the colonial charm of some of our more favored hotels here in the old city. The motel-style rooms have cable TV, minibar, and a/c. There is no Puerto Rican flair, to speak of, but the rooftop restaurant, though not renowned for its cuisine, does offer great panoramic views of Old San Juan (and has Internet access). Ask for a room in the back to cut down on street noise.

Howard Johnson Hotel Plaza de Armas, 202 Calle San José, Old San Juan, PR. ✆ 800-466-4656 or 787-722-9191, ✆ 787-725-3091, 🖵 www.hojo.com, plazadearmas@hotmail.com
💲 **Not So Cheap** 🍴 **CP** **CC** 51 rooms

What was once the funky Plaza de Armas has now been taken over and spruced up a bit by Howard Johnson. Being right on the plaza of the same name, this hotel is perfectly located. The rooms are not elegant, but all have a/c, cable TV, and Wi-Fi. HoJo invested about $400,000 for remodeling parts of the inn, including the dark lobby and the inclusion of a wine bar in the atrium, so hopefully this hotel will see brighter days.

La Caleta Guesthouse, Calle de las Monjas, Old San Juan, PR. ℭ 787-725-5347, ✆ 787-977-5642, 🖳 www.caletarealty.com, reservations@thecaleta.com

💲 **Not So Cheap** 🍴 **EP** CC 15 rooms

We have listed La Caleta for those who are looking to spend a little more time in Old San Juan. Though billed as a guesthouse, La Caleta is much more of a short-term vacation rental. The rooms are housed in a colonial three-story building on a quiet street close to the bay. All the apartments have kitchenettes, but they vary greatly in the range of amenities offered — some have TV, phone, and a/c, whereas others are much more basic. The two top-floor rooms are appealing — their bedrooms have a/c and the balconies have choice views. Keep in mind that this is not a hotel — there is no maid service, restaurant, or semblance of a front desk. However, for those looking to find their way and live like a true resident, La Caleta offers some great apartments, with rates from three nights to a month. The Sunshine Suite on the top floor has themed rooms with brushed pastel walls, a small sofa bed, and a TV. The bedroom is very simple, with a small bed and a/c.

Where to Eat

San Juan is a big city, and there are restaurants galore — from very expensive chichi bistros to the little snack bar on the street. By all means leave your hotel and sample and experience. We've tried to weed through the myriad of choices and to provide a good cross-section of the San Juan dining scene. Old San Juan seems to be the happening place in dining and should definitely be explored, but other parts of the city also hold their own, so you will never be far from a good restaurant.

Keep in mind that all the large hotels and resorts now have several restaurants that offer a variety of international cuisine. Although the food at many of these resorts is good, the one thing they all have in common is that they are very expensive, even overpriced. However, if you're staying in Dorado, for example, which is a 45-minute

drive from town, you might have to bite the bullet and eat at your hotel for sheer convenience. If you're staying right in San Juan, why sit
home? Get thee out and about!

Here are our suggestions.

Old San Juan

$$$$ **Aguaviva**, 364 Calle Fortaleza, 722-0665
Ever wonder what it would be like to eat in an underwater
restaurant? Well, in this ultra-chic spot featuring seaside
Latino cuisine, the fantasy comes to life. The style is impec-
cable, with turquoise floors, tables, and walls, accented by
white trim and hanging neon *aguavivas* ("jellyfish"). The food
is even better than the décor. The seviches are fantastic — try
the mahi mango lime or tuna and salmon sashimi duo. The
seared halibut medallions with crabmeat fondue and spinach
is quite savory, as are the wide array of oysters and special
seafood towers. Open for lunch from 11:30 a.m. to 4 p.m. and
for dinner from 6 to 11 p.m. No reservations are accepted, so
expect a wait.

$$$ **Amadeus**, 106 Calle San Sebastian, 722-8635
Right in the heart of Old San Juan, this famous intellectual
meeting spot serves all kinds of Puerto Rican and Caribbean
cuisine with a nouvelle flair. We adore the romantic candlelit
dining room in back and love the food, especially its delicacies
like risotto de mar with salmon and calamari. Open from noon
to 1 a.m.; no lunch on Monday. Reservations are suggested.

$$$$ **Barú**, 150 Calle San Sebastian, 977-5442
Set in a building dating back 250 years, Barú is a great place
to soak up some atmosphere along with some tasty fare. Sig-
nore Bignami, Barú's Italian chef, offers exciting Caribbean-
Mediterranean fusion cuisine, such as pork ribs with a ginger-
tamarindo glaze or our favorite — crab cakes topped with
seared scallops and a coconut curry sauce. There is an elegant
art-filled dining room, although we prefer the romantic court-
yard. The bar, complete with soothing lounge music, is a well-
frequented spot for the local young professional crowd. Open

for dinner from 5 p.m. to midnight (sometimes later) and on Sunday from 4 to 10 p.m.

$$ ★ **Café Berlin,** 407 Calle San Francisco, 722-5205
If you're looking for vegetarian or lighter and healthier fare, this is a fine and hip place for breakfast, lunch, and dinner. It's not at all expensive, and the Caribbean and international offerings include great breads, salads, and desserts. Vegetarians can try the tofu steak. If you just want coffee or herbal tea, this is the place. Open until 10 p.m. daily.

$$$ **Casa Borinquen,** 109 Calle San Sebastian, 722-7070
This quietly elegant nouvelle Latino restaurant on a peaceful side street is a pleasant, unassuming spot with a varied menu and an alfresco bar. The cream of yautia is a local specialty, served with chorizo bruschetta. For cheeseheads, the fried Puerto Rican cheese with guava rum sauce is worth a try. Entrees range from pasta (roasted pumpkin and macadamia ravioli) to meat and seafood (ahi tuna with garlic spinach). With candlelit tables, smooth jazz, and chandeliers, the small dining room is intimate, and the outdoor bar in back is a great place for an open-air cocktail. Open 6 p.m. until 1 a.m.; closed on Sunday.

$$$$ ★ **Dragonfly,** 364 Calle Fortaleza, 977-3886
This hot must-visit Asian eatery is across the street from the Parrot Club, and it's owned by the same entrepreneur, Robert Trevino. There are only seven tables, and no reservations are taken (expect a wait). It offers a community table option, or patrons can dine at the bar. The room is painted deep red and appointed in assorted chinoiserie. The music is from the Buddha Bar, and the gorgeous waitresses wear long silk dresses slit up the leg. It's got sex appeal to spare, but the food is also indelible: Peking duck nachos, rock shrimp tempura tacos, quesadilla spring rolls, seviche in coconut milk and ginger, and—well, you get the idea. The sake martinis are wicked good, and the chocolate pot de crème is our favorite dessert in all of Puerto Rico—indulge! Open 6 p.m. until midnight; closed on Sunday.

$$ **El Picoteo,** Hotel El Convento, 100 Calle Cristo, 723-9202
The best place for drinks in Old San Juan, El Picoteo serves tapas and light fare and is a symphony of connecting arches and tones of burnt sienna. We recommend its renowned grilled mushrooms and the baby eels (which were quite pricey). For those who don't want to take the tapas route, the mixed paella is a heftier selection. Open for lunch and dinner; closed on Monday.

$$$$ ⊛ **Il Perugino,** 105 Calle Cristo, 722-5481
Old San Juan's best Italian cuisine is served in this old colonial building that dates back more than two centuries. Specialties include carpaccios, homemade pastas, and a superb wine cellar. Come see why this is an award winner. Open for lunch and dinner until 11 p.m.; closed Sunday.

$$ **La Bombonera,** 259 Calle San Francisco, 722-0658
An institution in Old San Juan—it has been open for over a century—this is a great place for cheap Puerto Rican food when you're in the historic district. It's packed at lunchtime. It's also reputed to have the best Puerto Rican coffee in town. Open daily from 7:30 a.m. to 8:30 p.m.

$$$$$ La Chaumiére, 367 Calle Tetuán, 722-3330, 787-724-6034, or 787-977-0681
Right at the entrance to Old San Juan, Chef Didier welcomes guests from the world over. If you want French Provençal cuisine, this is San Juan's best. It's also one of San Juan's most elegant and most expensive restaurants. The scallops provençale will not disappoint. Reservations are advised. Open for dinner only; closed Sunday.

$$ **La Fonda del Jibarto,** 280 Calle del Sol, 725-8375
Once we visited this local favorite, we learned that thousands of Sanjuaneros can't be wrong! With its fun atmosphere and hearty tasty *criollo* cuisine, this laid-back family-run spot has been packing them in for years. When you ask what is best on the menu, they will say, "*Todo!*" We can't argue. Open 10 a.m. to 9 p.m. daily.

$$$ **La Mallorquina,** 207 Calle San Justo, 722-3261
This is a fine old-style restaurant that serves Puerto Rican and Spanish specialties (try the *asopao*—a Puerto Rican rice dish). Set in an old building with murals and ceiling fans, this is a very pleasant place for lunch. It is San Juan's oldest restaurant and has been owned and operated by the same family since 1848. It's open for lunch and dinner, but it is most popular as a lunch spot. Closed Sunday.

$$$ **Makario's,** 361 Calle Tetuan, 723-8653
Arab chef Oliver Makario offers contemporary Arab Mediterranean cuisine in this Egyptian-owned eatery. For an authentic taster, we recommend the vegetarian platter—a hearty mix of falafel, baba ghanoush, and tabouli served with pita bread. The grilled halibut filet with mango sauce is a good bet for those who aren't into the traditional Arab options (such as stuffed grape leaves, shish kebabs, or falafel). We recommend this place on weekends, when the cozy upstairs den features a belly dancer. Open noon until 11 p.m.

$$$$ ✪ **The Parrot Club,** 363 Calle Fortaleza, 725-7370
One of the hottest restaurants in town is chef Robert Trevino's Parrot Club, featuring *nuevo latino* cuisine—best described as a mélange of Puerto Rican and other Latino dishes. Colorful and lively, the restaurant and its popular bar are always packed. The *bocalitos* with spicy crab salad make a wonderful appetizer, and the seared sea bass with lobster and scallop confit will satisfy any seafood lover. Meat eaters will love the roast pork served with cranberry salsa. One of the sides offered is a *torta* made with goat cheese, grilled portabellos, and sweet plantains—gotta try it to believe it. With live music, the Parrot Club is ideal for those seeking a taste of Puerto Rican flair. Open for lunch and dinner every day, and open until midnight Thursday through Saturday.

$$$ ✪ **Sake,** 305 Calle Recinto Sur, 977-1082
San Juan continues to go upscale, as this stylish sushi restaurant proves. The design here is simply sensational, with three different ambiances. The front room (the Lotus Room) is more

of a lounge, although we wish we could hang out on the circular couches all night. The main dining room is a little chilly, but the back room, the actual sushi bar, is more laid back and fun. The menu includes imaginative twists on hot apps and sushi rolls. The impressive drink menu includes special sushi wine from France. For groups, the Japanese-style VIP table is a must—it has great style and fabulous presentation. Open from 6 to 11 p.m.; closed Monday and Tuesday.

$$$ **Sofia**, 355 Calle San Francisco, 721-0396
The latest of Robert Trevino's creations, this Italian restaurant has won over stomachs in a short time. The Latino Bellini (mango juice and prosecco) whets any appetite, as does the grilled shrimp and eggplant appetizer. The pastas here are the specialty—baked ziti with four-cheese sauce, or our favorite, linguini with clams, pancetta, and pepperocini. Open 6 p.m. to midnight.

$$$$ **Tantra**, 356 Calle Fortaleza, 977-8141
Old San Juan finally has an Indian restaurant, but judging from the menu and its Indo-Latino vibe, this is not pure Indian cuisine. The East Indian pork with yogurt risotto is a perfect marriage between the two, as are many of the tasty appetizers. Open for lunch and dinner, with a belly dancer Thursday through Saturday.

Condado

$$$ ⊛ **Ajili Mójili**, 1006 Avenida Ashford, 725-9195
This is the best place in San Juan to sample authentic Puerto Rican cuisine. The restaurant, in a new, larger location, is very attractive and full of locals, so you know it's good. There's great service, too. Try the *mofongo* or the salmon skewers wrapped with bacon. The *tostones*, another Puerto Rican specialty, are excellent. Keep your eyes open for celebs. Open for lunch and dinner (on Saturday for dinner only). Reservations are suggested.

$$$$ **Cherry Blossom**, 1309 Avenida Ashford, 723-7300
This Japanese steak and seafood restaurant offers teppanyaki dining, with the chef at the table slicing and dicing his way through three courses. Choose shrimp, steak, or scallop, and watch him go to work. It also offers a great selection of sushi. Open daily for lunch and dinner; no lunch on Saturday.

$$$$$ **Ramiro's**, 1106 Avenida Magdalena, 721-9049, 721-9056, or 722-6067
Serving delicious international cuisine with Spanish Castilian flourishes (dubbed "New Creole"), the Ramiro brothers create food that is as pretty to look at as it is good to eat. Closed for lunch on Saturday. Reservations are suggested.

$$ **Vía Appia**, 1350 Avenida Ashford, 725-8711
If you want southern Italian cuisine (lasagna, baked ziti, spaghetti, eggplant parmesan) and pizza, this is a pleasant place to sit and eat under the awning in front. Although the service can be slow and at times indifferent, the food is hearty and the price is right. Open daily for lunch and dinner.

$ **Waikiki**, 1025 Avenida Ashford, 977-2267 or 977-2266
This super-casual place looks like nothing special from the street, but those in the know pass through to the picturesque deck overlooking the Caribbean Sea. We love to come here and nosh on some marlin nuggets and have a rum and Coke. Though enjoyable in the sun, this place is even better on those humid nights, as the sea breeze provides natural air-conditioning. Open from 11 a.m. to midnight Monday through Friday and 8 a.m. to midnight on the weekend.

$$$ **Yerba Buena**, 1350 Avenida Ashford, 721-5700
With creative Caribbean cuisine and streetside dining right on the main drag, this bistro-style spot offers up a tasty blend of entrées. Try the rack of lamb in guava rum sauce. Yerba Buena also has live Cuban music on Thursday and Sunday. Open from 6 p.m. to midnight and until 2 a.m. on the weekend; open Sunday from 5 to 11 p.m.

Isla Verde

$$ **Casa Dante**, 39 Calle Loíza, 726-7310
This bustling family spot on the main drag specializes in *mo-fongos*. For those who don't know, *mofongo* is a famous *boricua* (native) dish. Casa Dante is the perfect place to sample these mashed plantains, which are stuffed with meat or seafood and topped with red sauce.

$$$ **Mares,** Ritz-Carlton Hotel, 6961 Avenida de los Gobernadores, 253-1700
This casual restaurant in the Ritz-Carlton is a consistent spot for well-prepared food using regional recipes and spices. It offers indoor or alfresco dining. We prefer the Caribbean buffets offered for breakfast and lunch, and we warn readers that the Friday night Seafood Extravaganza is in fact extravagant! For an à la carte option, try the surf 'n' turf or the red snapper in a banana leaf and served with *fufu* and *criollo* sauce. The guava crème brûlée is divine. Open daily for lunch and dinner.

$$$ **Pescadería Atlántica**, 2475 Calle Loíza, Punta Las Marías, 726-6654
In a new and bigger location, this is the place to go if you want really fresh seafood at reasonable prices. This is a popular spot with locals at lunch and dinner. Don't expect a fancy restaurant, just fresh fish. Open from noon to 10 p.m. Closed Sunday.

$$$ ✹ **Ruth's Chris Steak House**, Inter-Continental San Juan Resort and Casino, 5961 Avenida Isla Verde, 791-6100
Even with such a difficult name to pronounce, Ruth's Chris is renowned as the best steak joint in the city. If you crave beef, this is the place. Its steaks are cooked in its signature 1,800°F oven. The New Orleans–inspired appetizers like barbequed shrimp are a great start. Open for dinner.

$$$$ **Tangerine**, in San Juan Water & Beach Club Hotel, 2 Calle José Tartak, 728-3666
Searching for chic dining? Look no farther. Local chef Nelson

Rosado welcomes you to the sexy San Juan Water & Beach Club Hotel for a sensuous dining experience where even the menu is loaded with sexual innuendos. The cuisine is a Caribbean-Asian fusion, with succulent appetizers such as the geisha seviche with lobster and green onion. The entrees are just as good—we loved the rack of lamb with tamarindo sauce, as well as the red snapper. And who can pass up the orgasm cheesecake, which is fried and topped with home-made vanilla bean ice cream and ginger marmalade? With water-filled glass walls and sleek design, the décor fits into the seduction theme of the hotel, and the food is fantastic as well. Open for dinner until 11 p.m.

Ocean Park

$–$$$ ✪ **Hostería del Mar,** 1 Calle Tapia, 727-3302
This is one of the best spots for lunch in San Juan. You dine in a wooden pavilion with windows open to the beach and the trade winds. The service is lacking but the menu is rich, from macrobiotic and vegetarian to *criollo* and chicken and fish dishes. There are also great sandwiches. It's good for breakfast ($), lunch ($$), and dinner ($$$).

$ ✪ **Kasalta Bakery,** 1966 Calle McLeary, 727-7340
An institution in Ocean Park, this very popular local bakery and cafeteria eatery for breakfast, lunch, and dinner serves the best café con leche in town. The prices are really cheap here, too. Lunch and dinner specials include Puerto Rican dishes (*caldo gallego*, for instance) that are completely unknown to non-Latinos. Also popular are the Cuban sandwiches—a meal in themselves. Open daily from 6 a.m. till 10 p.m. A definite must-stop!

$$$$ ✪ **Pamela's Caribbean Cuisine,** Numero Uno on the Beach, 1 Calle Santa Ana, 728-3379 or 726-5010
Executive chef Esteban Torres continues the excellent cuisine of this beachside restaurant, which has created quite a stir in restaurant-rich San Juan. Pamela's also now has a/c, more

space, and a view of the beach from every table (the wall on the beach has been opened up). Service may be a tad slow, but the fusion of Caribbean and international cuisine and the use of fresh island produce and seafood make for a wonderful dining experience. ¡*Sabroso*! Open daily for lunch (noon to 3 p.m.) and dinner (7 to 10:30 p.m.). It now offers tapas from 3 to 7 p.m. Reservations suggested.

$$$$ **Ristorante Casa di Legno**, 1130 Avenida Roosevelt, 273-1584
This is a wonderful Italian restaurant in the old Mona's space. Chef Pierre St. Hubert has created one of San Juan's best-kept secrets, with more than 40 choices of pasta, seafood, and meat dishes. Closed Monday.

Miramar

$$$$ **Augosto's Cuisine**, Courtyard by Marriott San Juan Miramar, 801 Avenida Ponce de León, 725-7700
A favorite restaurant of well-to-do locals, Augosto's features one of the finest chefs on the island. The cuisine is classic European, and the menu changes frequently. The dining room is an elegant setting with plenty of flowers. Reservations are suggested.

$$$$ **Chayote**, Olimpo Court Hotel, 603 Avenida Miramar, 722-9385
This is consistently rated one of San Juan's best dining experiences. Chef Alfredo Ayala merges Caribbean, Puerto Rican, and international cuisine in such a delicious way that Chayote is the delight of in-the-know locals. Be sure to save room for dessert here. Reservations are a must. Open Tuesday through Friday for lunch and dinner, and Saturday for dinner.

Puerto Nuevo

$$ **Aurorita's**, 303 Avenida de Diego, 783-2899
Good Mexican food, live mariachi music (Thursday through Sunday), and an out-of-the-way location (take a cab) make this a fun excursion. Closed Monday.

Santurce

$$ **Bebos Café,** 1600 Calle Loíza, 268-5087
If you're seeking an authentic Puerto Rican meal, head to this hot-spot in Santurce. Renowned for its *criollo* cuisine, Bebos is busy from morning to midnight. For those who haven't tried *mofongos,* this is another good spot to give it a go! Open daily from 7:30 a.m. until 12:30 a.m.

$$$ **La Casona,** 609 Calle San Jorge, 727-2717
Set within a colonial-period house, this restaurant is authentic in ambiance and cuisine. Traditional Spanish fare keeps customers coming back to this popular spot. Lunches cater to businesspeople looking for a hearty meal, whereas dinners are romantic affairs. The meats are exceptionally seasoned, especially the rack of lamb, which is a local favorite. Open for lunch and dinner; closed on Sunday.

$$$ **Las Tablas,** 166 Ponce de Léon, 977-5600 or -977-5601
Located next to the Luis A. Ferre Performing Arts Center, this stylish spot combines flavors from the Indians, Spanish conquistadors, and Africans. The result is delectable. We like to start with a drink on the patio and then enter the softly lit restaurant for dinner. It often has dancing later. For an unusual surf 'n' turf, we recommend the lamb chops in red wine sauce, complemented by langostinos in cilantro sauce.

$$$$ ⊛ **Pikayo,** Museum of Art, 299 Avenida de Diego, 721-6194
Housed in the Art Museum, this is an elegant yet relaxing place to sample celebrity chef Wilo Benet's "exotic Caribbean" cuisine (although we also saw traces of Chinese, Middle Eastern, French, and Thai, to name just a few). The creative dishes are presented so beautifully that it seems a shame to eat them —but we got over that feeling quickly! The menu changes frequently. We sampled the spicy tuna tartar with peanut sauce and the sea bass with Hawaiian purple mashed potatoes—they were both excellent. We love watching the action in the kitchen on the big TV screen placed over the bar. Come see

why this place was named one of the world's top 100 restaurants by *Condé Nast*. Open for dinner Monday through Saturday and for lunch on Tuesday through Friday; closed Sunday.

⊛ Going Out

Get out those cha-cha heels! With the best and greatest variety in the Caribbean, nightlife is why you stay in San Juan. There are lots of bars and clubs of all persuasions, and there is no set closing time. Most places close when the last person spins off the dance floor and stumbles onto the street. As in any city, weekend nights will be the busiest and most crowded in the clubs. Also, all clubs will usually have a cover charge of between $5 and $15 (especially on weekends), which usually includes at least one free drink. For those who like to gamble, all the big hotels in Condado and Isla Verde have casinos (the most glittering is the one at El San Juan in Isla Verde). So take your disco nap, strap on those sling-backs or put on those Pradas, and off you go into the night.

Straight Bars and Clubs

For years, two of the hottest clubs in San Juan have been Luxor (formerly called Stargate) and Club Lazer. But there is a new generation of clubs springing up, such as Milk and Club Liquid (not the former Liquid that was in the San Juan Water & Beach Club). Both of these nightclubs could easily be in Miami or New York. We've also listed some other choices in case you get tired of them and want a change of pace. Note that when going to the straight clubs here, people tend to get dressed up — that means no shorts, T-shirts, athletic shoes, or sandals for men (jeans are iffy; best to wear dressier pants); for women, dresses are preferred (the tighter and more leg showing, the better — remember, this is macho and sexist Latin America).

Blend, 309 Calle Fortaleza, Old San Juan, 977-7777
> On Thursday through Sunday, this bar turns into a thumping scene with electronica pulsing through the two rooms. There is never a cover, but dress elegantly. This gets crowded, but the dance energy is infectious. Open 11 p.m. until 4 a.m.

Club Brava, El San Juan Hotel, 6063 Avenida Isla Verde, Isla
  Verde, 791-2781
  This is actually two clubs in one, with *reggaetón* and hip-hop
  on the first floor and electronic music on the top floor. Although it attracts ultra-flashy types (perhaps too flashy for our
  taste), if you're looking for a big club experience in San Juan,
  Brava is it.

Club Lazer, 251 Calle Cruz, Old San Juan, 725-7581 or 721-4479
  This is San Juan's premier disco. For those who want to experience the *reggaetón* craze firsthand, head to Club Lazer. In
  this three-floor club, you'll hear all the current dance hits with
  all the high-tech accoutrements you expect in a hot club; there
  is also a roof-deck garden jungle. It's stylish, it's fun, and it
  gets packed.

Club Liquid, 1420 Avenida Ponce de León, Santurce, no phone
  info at press time
  Not to be confused with the former club called Liquid that
  was in the San Juan Water & Beach Club, this is a dressy disco
  that is popular with the local crowd. At press time, it was in
  the process of being transformed from the very popular
  Teatro (once the also popular Asylum). As before, it will have
  some live music, but it will mostly employ DJs to spin hot *reggaetón* and will be open (and crowded) from Thursday through
  Saturday.

Dunbar's, 1954 Calle McLedary, Ocean Park, 728-2920
  This is a casual, popular landmark in Ocean Park, packed
  with locals. It has live music on weekends and pool tables as
  well. Best of all, it's beachside.

⊛ **Luxor**, 1 Avenida Roberto H. Todd, Santurce, 721-6129
  Formerly called Stargate and located just south of Condado
  and the expressway, across the street from the fast-food plaza,
  this has for years been one of San Juan's premier clubs. It features several dance floors and lavish décor (which includes
  the hot clientele). The cover charge is usually around $10.

Maria's Bar, 204 Calle de Cristo, Old San Juan, 787-721-1678
  One of the oldest bars in San Juan, this institution offers an
  authentic look at Old San Juan's nightlife. Open from 11 a.m.
  until early morning.

Milk, 314 Calle Fortaleza, Old San Juan, 721-3548
  Places like this make it clear that San Juan has come into its
  own on the nightclub scene. Occupying the space of the former Ku Lounge and Kudetá Restaurant, this hot spot features
  DJs, dancing (mostly to house music), and lots of young hip-
  sters, all in an ultra-modern ambiance. The club takes up several floors and has several rooms of various themes. A state-
  of-the-art Kryiogenyx cooling system keeps things dry and
  comfy. There is a $10 cover charge. Open on the weekend un-
  til 5 a.m.

⊛ **Nuyorican Café**, 312 Calle San Francisco, Old San Juan, 977-1276
  This authentic spot is our favorite place for live music in San
  Juan. Located on a little side street, it has a great mixed crowd
  and a super-cool ambiance. There is live music every night
  and simple food, such as pizza and appetizers. Open from 7
  p.m. until late.

Parrot Club, 363 Calle Fortaleza, Old San Juan, 725-7370
  This restaurant gets very lively and crowded after the dinner
  crowd leaves (if it ever does). It often features fantastic live
  music. Open until 1 a.m.

San Juan Marriott, 1309 Avenida Ashford, Condado, 722-7000
  The lobby bar of the Marriott attracts a stylish crowd, especially on Wednesday through Sunday, with live salsa and mer-
  engue music—there is lots of dancing here.

Ventana al Mar, Avenida Ashford, Condado
  This little complex of bars on the coast looks out over a cute
  park and fountain and provides perfect vistas of the sea.
  These chic little bars are a great place to grab a cocktail in the
  fresh air. The action builds on weekends. It's good for those
  who are not interested in the club scene.

⊛ **Wet,** in San Juan Water & Beach Club Hotel, Isla Verde, 728-3666
This sexy lounge sits on the top floor of this hot boutique hotel.
It offers sushi for late diners, but many come to enjoy the intimate setting, plush poolside furniture, excellent evening
views, and smooth tunes played by a DJ. Open nightly until
late.

⊛ *Gay and Lesbian Bars and Clubs*

San Juan has the best, and pretty much only, gay and lesbian nightlife in the Caribbean. Although there is a little nightlife scene in
Santo Domingo in the Dominican Republic, San Juan is it until you
get as far south as Caracas, Venezuela. There even used to be a gay
newspaper here, *Puerto Rico Breeze,* which lasted several years before
ceasing publication in the fall of 2006. Many of the gay clubs in
Puerto Rico are mixed gay and lesbian, especially outside San Juan.
And most clubs, it seems, are dropping the "gay" and "straight" la-
bels altogether. You'll find many of both, no matter where you go
dancing in San Juan. There are frequently gay nights at many of the
straight clubs (which change constantly). For those looking for the
"bathhouse" experience, **Steamworks**'s San Juan location was per-
manently closed in 2006. However, this popular gym, sauna, and
entertainment spot has plans to reopen as soon as it finds an appropriate place on the island. So, Steamworks aside, here are some good
options.

Atlantic Beach Bar, 1 Calle Vendig, Condado, 721-6900
This is the happy-hour spot from 4 to 6 p.m. Monday
through Saturday. Sunday is dance night and the post–beach
day crowd gathers in the late afternoon and stays until the
early morning. Although there no longer are special shows
on Sunday, it is still the strongest night.

The Faktory Club, 1412 Avenida Ponce de Léon, Santurce, 724-9083.
Another of the popular newer gay bars in San Juan, The Faktory Club (formerly Nuestro Ambiente up until spring 2007)
is recognized as the best (or, at least, it stays open the latest)
late-night spot in town.

Junior's Bar, 613 Calle Condado, Santurce, 723-9477

Open nightly, this isn't a big hitter on the gay scene, but this cozy bar is a fun spot (mostly for locals) to just hang out and listen or dance to salsa music. There are also strippers on most nights.

⊛ **Krash Klub**, 1257 Avenida Ponce de Léon, Santurce, 722-1131 or www.krashpr.com

Eros was remodeled in 2007 and became Krash Klub (which had actually been its first name prior to becoming Eros). Whatever. Name confusion aside, this is still the hottest gay club in San Juan (and, perhaps, the best dance club in the city). It is located next to the Metro Theater and just around the corner from Luxor. The DJ spins world-class house music, and there are often shows starting around 1 a.m. Wednesday is hip-hop and *reggaetón*; Thursday and Friday are house or tribal; Saturday is mixed '70s to '90s tunes; Sunday is hip-hop and Latin.

Medusa, 7 Avenida Roosevelt, Hato Rey, 787-764-9230 or www.medusatheclub.com

This vintage 2006 club has fast become one of the hotter spots on the gay scene. It's a casual and comfortable atmosphere, but revelers tend to dress fashionably as they dance on two floors to house, techno, R&B, hip-hop, and Latin rythyms well into the morning. There are also several theme parties and a variety of performers.

Starz, 365 Avenida de Diego & Ponce de Léon, Santurce, 721-8645 or www.starzclub.com

This new club is a popular late-night weekend spot and includes a pulsing dance floor, a lounge area, and a terrace that sits under the "starz." There is no shortage of scantily clad dancers, and while we're heading in that direction, there is also an occasional strip-shower show. Dress to impress.

Tropical, 1708 Calle San Mateo, Santurce, 268-3570

A predominantly lesbian club, Tropical is the new improved and remodeled version of what was once called Cups at the

Barn. Cups had been around since the 1980s and was always the place to be. Tropical, which opened in summer 2007, figures to be every bit as good as its prior self. Wednesday and Friday are usually the big nights here.

THE NORTH COAST

Dorado

The name *Dorado*, or "Golden," might come from the name of an influential family from the 1500s or from the golden sand beaches here. Whatever the origin, Dorado is regarded today as one of the premier ★golf resorts in the Caribbean. Since this was developed as a resort town, there is not much to do here besides golf and hang out at the beach (although there is a pleasant plaza with a statue paying homage to the Taíno Indians, the Spanish conquistador, and the African slaves). Two sister resorts, built by the Rockefellers' Rock-Resorts company in 1958 (Dorado Beach) and 1972 (Cerromar Beach) and purchased by the Hyatt in 1985, share a 1,000-acre former grapefruit and coconut plantation just west of the town of Dorado and 22 miles west of San Juan. Unfortunately, the Cerromar has been converted into a time-share called Hyatt Hacienda del Mar Vacation Club Resort, and the Hyatt Dorado Beach ceased operations in May 2006. The Hyatt Hacienda del Mar will accept some bookings like a regular hotel, but only on a limited basis. As for the Hyatt Dorado Beach, the Puerto Rico Tourism Company has hopes that a new owner will step forward and renovate the outdated facility, but there is nothing in the works to suggest that this will happen in the near future.

Despite the aforementioned changes, the four 18-hole Championship golf courses (some of the best in the Caribbean) remain open. Thus, Dorado is still a golfer's paradise. The four 18-hole Robert Trent Jones II Championship courses (called East, West, Pineapple, and Sugarcane) are on flat and rolling terrain that will challenge all golfers. They have been the site of numerous golf tournaments. All

feature Mr. Jones's trademarks: huge greens, lots of bunkers and water hazards, and long fairways. Probably the toughest links are the East
and West courses. The **East**, at 6,985 yards, has the super-tough 13th
hole, a double-dogleg, 540-yard, two-pond nightmare. The **West**, at
6,913 yards, has the toughest par-3s at the resort, spiting you with
sloping greens and *muchos* bunkers. Both the Pineapple and Sugarcane courses were redesigned in 2004. The **Pineapple** (formerly
known as North) course is a 6,620-yard links-style course, and the
Sugarcane (formerly known as South), at 6,571 yards, is a challenge
of winds and mega water hazards. Greens fees are $195 (but only
$105 after 1 p.m.) and include carts. Club rentals are $55. For tee
times, call 797-796-1234.

Where to Stay

Hyatt Hacienda del Mar Vacation Club Resort, 301 Highway 693,
    Dorado, PR. 𝄞 787-796-3000, ✎ 787-796-3610,
    ⌨ www.hyatthaciendadelmar.hyatt.com

🍸 **Ridiculous** and up 🍽 **EP** **CC** 160 rooms

> Hacienda del Mar is a multiwinged seven-story building with
> a big-resort feel (the lobby looks much like an airline termi-
> nal). Now that its primary function is as a time-share, it has
> very limited availability and doesn't quite have the energy that
> the Cerromar once had. However, families still love this place,
> with its huge River Pool complex, expansive beach (beware
> the often strong undertow), and activities geared for adults
> and kids of all ages. One of Hacienda del Mar's unique fea-
> tures is the River Pool — at 1,776 feet long, it's said to be the
> longest current-propelled pool in the world (but who's check-
> ing on those things?). It moves water at 22,600 gallons per
> minute and has 14 waterfalls and 4 water slides. The slide, at
> its conclusion, is three stories high and requires stairs to
> climb, but it is a blast. Be prepared to get a noseful of water
> from the splashdown (we did). Although the whole River Pool
> idea is contrived (it was added in the '80s to attract families
> and vacationers who like the mega-resorts), it is different and

fun, and both adults and kids will enjoy it (there is a bar with barstools in the water about halfway down, for a quick piña colada). There are five restaurants and bars, a casino, eight tennis courts, and a business center on the property.

All rooms at Hacienda del Mar face the ocean. Most are very comfortable studio apartments with well-equipped kitchens or kitchenettes. They are attractively furnished, with marble baths, a/c, voicemail, high-speed Internet, cable TV, VCR, stereo, room safes (and safe deposit boxes at the front desk), minibars, irons, and ironing boards. Some rooms have data ports.

Unfortunately, the once-popular kids club, Camp Hyatt, has been nixed, and, gasp, there is no longer any room service — a definite negative.

Embassy Suites Dorado del Mar Beach & Golf Resort, 201 Dorado del Mar Boulevard, Dorado, PR. 𝄐 800-EMBASSY or 787-796-6125, 📞 787-796-6145 🖳 www.embassysuites.hilton.com
💲 **Very Pricey** 🍴 **BP** CC 210 suites

It seems that the Hilton has successfully muscled in on what was once the Hyatt's territory, as this new Embassy Suites suggests. Although this hotel complex looks enormous (and certainly boasts one heck of a long name), one of the huge buildings is a time-share associated with the hotel. As usual, all rooms here are suites and include a big living room with a fridge, a microwave, two TVs, a phone with voicemail, and high-speed Internet access. The bedrooms resemble an Embassy Suites in Louisville or elsewhere. The kitchenette has microwave, coffeemaker, and fridge. The lagoon pool is built over the ocean and is home to the Blue Seahorse Bar and Grill. There is also the run-of-the-mill, always open, casual Paradise Restaurant, which is hardly paradisiacal. The hotel's Italian restaurant offering is called Oregano — it overlooks a golf course. Speaking of golf (and who isn't, when it comes to Dorado?), there is a putting green and a driving range, as well as access to the courses here in Dorado. We like the cook-to-order breakfast, but this resort is a bit of a cookie-cutter variety.

THE NORTHEAST COAST

Río Grande and Río Mar

Located 19 traffic-prone miles east of San Juan's international airport and just west of the pretty and popular (with locals) Luquillo beaches are Río Grande and its Río Mar development. Río Grande was once full of sugar and coffee plantations, but now it is known for its imports—rich tourists. In this once sleepy part of Puerto Rico, the mid-1990s saw the rapid development of the 451-acre Río Mar Resort, swallowing up a mile of pristine beach with a big resort hotel, two golf courses, and condo developments. However, we weren't terribly impressed with the look and design of the resort.

Río Mar is very close to El Yunque National Forest (see the Don't Miss section at the end of this chapter) and the Fajardo marina mecca on the east coast. Minutes away is Luquillo Beach, one of the best in all of Puerto Rico. Once a coconut plantation, and now a still majestic beach shaded by palms, it is a fun place at which to hang out and commune with *puertorriqueños*. For a little adventure, we recommend a kayak trip with **Aqua Frenzy** (741-0913). It has both single and double kayaks and runs guided trips.

Luquillo also has Puerto Rico's first wheelchair-accessible beach recreational facility. There is a ramp system from the parking lot right into the water, as well as wheelchair-accessible restrooms. For more information on Luquillo wheelchair facilities, call Compania Parque Nacional at 787-622-5200.

Where to Stay

Wyndham Río Mar Beach Resort & Spa, 6000 Río Mar Boulevard, Río Grande, PR. ✆ 877-999-3223, 800-474-6627, or 787-888-6000, ✉ 787-888-6600, 🖥 www.wyndham.com

💲 **Ridiculous** and up 🍴 **EP** CC 600 rooms

In May 2007, Wyndham took over the Río Mar Beach Resort & Spa, which sprawls along the beach in a very long, multi-storied, and rather architecturally bland building. Fifty-eight ocean villa suites were built next to the main hotel and opened in 2000. It's popular for its convention facilities (with a whopping 48,000 square feet available) as well as its two Championship 18-hole golf courses (designed by the Fazio Brothers and Greg Norman) that spread out behind and around the hotel, but we find this to be just another big, expensive, and boring place to stay. True, golfers and expense-accounters will love it, and there are a slew of other activities. These include 13 Har-Tru ✪tennis courts (four lighted), a spa and fitness facility, water sports and a dive center, three beachfront pools, a kids' club, a daily activities calendar, and (yawn) the requisite casino. Far more appealing to us is its proximity to El Yunque and San Juan (but we'd rather stay in San Juan — that's just our personal preference). The palm-lined beach is pretty, but it can get a tad rough. The sand here is coarse and a light shade of brown (i.e., it is not a white-sand beach).

Things get better on the inside. The rooms are new and close to the sea. We like that oceanside guests can open their slider and hear the surf. The golf course side has very pretty views of the almost perpetually cloud-topped El Yunque summit and the mountains around it. The room décor is attractive and colorful. All have lanais; a/c; Internet; phones with voicemail, data port, and conference-calling ability; minibars and coffeemakers; TVs with in-room movies; Nintendo; video account review and checkout; and irons and ironing boards. We like that the Wyndham has 24-hour room service, since we'll be hungry after a night out on the town. The hotel also has a business center with Wi-Fi, and, count 'em, 11 restaurants, as well as a slew of bar possibilities. Look for packages and corporate discounts.

Gran Meliá Puerto Rico, P.O. Box 43006, Playa Coco, Río Grande, PR. ⓒ 888-95-MELIA or 787-809-1770, ✆ 787-809-1785, 🖳 www.granmeliapuertorico.com, gran.melia.puerto.rico@solmelia.com

💲 **Beyond Belief** ⑪ **All-Inclusive** 🆑 486 rooms

The latest addition to the chain owned by Spanish giant Meliá

Hotels is this monstrous resort built on the Miquillo Península. Although it's billed as a "tropical oasis of elegance and fun," we don't see much more than a super-pricey all-inclusive resort, but beauty is in the eye of the beholder. For those who seek pampering at a high level of comfort—and are prepared to pay for it—this chic resort fits the bill. The lagoon-style swimming pool is perched next to a beautiful beach close to Río Grande. The pool has a swim-up bar and is especially beautiful when illuminated at night. The resort features all the typical amenities. Gran Meliá is known for casino, water sports, nightly entertainment, "daily activities," two golf courses, tennis courts, spa, and health club. There are different classes of rooms, but all have 25-inch cable TV, Internet access, alarm clock, minibar, hairdryer, coffeemaker, and room service. We prefer the suites here, which are housed in individual two-story bungalows and include separate living rooms and veranda. The Royal Service—including personal butler service, breakfast and snacks in a private area, and newspaper service—is a bit over-the-top and not worth the hefty price of an upgrade. Besides the El Mirador buffet on the beach, the Gran Meliá offers five à la carte restaurants with cuisine options such as Californian, sushi, or Italian. Be warned—this place is expensive!

Fajardo

The northeast corner of Puerto Rico has the huge Roosevelt Roads U.S. Naval Station, El Yunque National Forest, and the bustling town of Fajardo—a major marina area for boats due to its proximity to the marine playground of several Puerto Rican islands, cays, and the Virgin Islands. There is not much in Fajardo itself, which is why we find it quite humorous that locals often refer to it as the Metropolis of the East. In fact, it seems that most people come to Fajardo in order to leave, because this is where ferries and most scheduled air services depart for Culebra and Vieques. Due to traffic, the drive from San Juan can take an hour to an hour and a half. Just north of Fajardo, on the bluffs of Las Croabas, is the gigantic El Conquistador Resort &

Golden Door Spa. Fajardo is a great place from which to take day trips—there are great spots for scuba diving as well as snorkeling. For those who are into aquatic sports, **Island Kayaking Adventure** (462-7204) runs great trips from Fajardo.

Where to Stay

In addition to the hotels listed below, Fajardo has one of Puerto Rico's best camp sites, **Seven Seas** (787-863-8180), which has room for 500 tents and basic facilities, as well as a restaurant.

Fajardo Inn, P.O. Box 4309, 52 Parcelas Beltran, Puerto Real, PR.
  ☎ 888-860-6006 or 787-860-6000, ✉ 787-860-5063,
  🖥 www.fajardoinn.com, info@fajardoinn.com
💲 **Not So Cheap** 🍴 **EP** CC 100 rooms

Since so many tourists pass through Fajardo on their way to and from Vieques and Culebra, we were eager to find a hotel more suited to our readers' taste than the over-the-top El Conquistador. Luckily, we found a hidden gem. The Fajardo Inn is located on a hilltop minutes outside town, offering exquisite views of the ocean and of El Yunque National Rainforest. Travelers who aren't planning on visiting the forest can at least take a good look from here. The hotel has been vastly improved with the recent addition of Coco's Park water park, a sprawling complex of pools, complete with a waterslide, Jacuzzi, swim-up bar, tennis court, and, yes, the highlight of anybody's trip to Puerto Rico—a miniature golf course. The inn is housed in a plantation-style stucco building, replete with an elegant spiral staircase. There are three on-site restaurants to choose from, the best of which is the award-winning Star Fish Restaurant—it offers a fusion of *criollo* cuisine specializing in seafood. Recently, the inn opened up a fitness center and a tennis court. Plans are in the works to add more rooms.

The rooms are equipped with a/c, cable TV, and queen-size beds. This inn has the amenities of a resort but still retains the ambiance of an inn. We still prefer to stay along the coast, but if you're looking to break up a trip to or from one of the islands off the coast, a layover at the Fajardo Inn might be just the solution.

El Conquistador Resort & Golden Door Spa, 1000 Avenida Conquistador, Fajardo, PR. ☎ 866-317-8932 or 787-863-1000, ✆ 787-863-6500, 🖳 www.elconresort.com

💲 **Wicked Pricey** and up 🍴 **EP** 🆔 983 rooms

With more than 500 acres, nearly 1,000 rooms and suites, an acclaimed Arthur Hill 18-hole golf course, seven tennis courts (four lighted), six swimming pools, a marina, all kinds of water sports (including a dive shop), its own private island with beaches, chaises, horseback riding, a fitness center, nine restaurants, eight bars, a shopping arcade, a casino, and even a funicular to climb part of the 300-foot bluff over which the hotel is sprawled, El Conquistador Resort & Golden Door Spa is the biggest hotel in Puerto Rico. Indeed, it can take 20 minutes just to walk from top to bottom. As if the resort weren't already loaded with facilities, a new water park will be "making waves" here in the winter of 2008. The hotel has four distinct guest wings or buildings. At the top of the hill is the La Vista Wing, midway down the hill is the Las Brisas Wing (where we stayed), and at the bottom of the hill near or on the water are Las Olas and La Marina Villages. Adjacent to the La Vista Wing is Las Casitas, which has 90 luxury villas with a price tag to match. The first Golden Door Spa in the Caribbean is also located there.

Although it is a tad large for our taste (bigger isn't always better), El Conquistador will appeal to those who want a self-contained resort with lots of options and activities. Most of the hotel's activities are on the top of the hill, including the soaring lobby and the casino. Also on top is the striking main pool area featuring several levels, three pools (including a lap pool), columns, palm trees, and fab views. Those who want to be near them should consider staying in La Vista or Las Brisas. The yellow-tone décor of the rooms is quite nice and a refreshing change from pastels. All rooms have lanais, a/c, Internet access, three multilined phones with voicemail, two

TVs with movie channels and VCR, bars, safes, fridges, irons and ironing boards, and good-size baths. But what we really loved was the stereo system with three-disc CD and dual-cassette player—a rarity in any big resort.

We didn't like three things about the resort. We found the dining experience to be unexceptional and very expensive— even with nine choices. Given the location, going out to dine in Fajardo is inconvenient. We also did not like having to schlep to Palomino Island by scheduled water taxi (it leaves every 30 minutes between 9 a.m. and 4 p.m.—the last taxi returns at 6 p.m.). It's bad enough just getting to the bottom of the hill! Finally, though exclusively used by hotel guests, the 100-acre island has a small swimming beach that can get crowded. It had lots of seaweed in the water when we were there. Look for packages and corporate discounts.

Las Casitas Village & Golden Door Spa, 1000 Avenida Conquistador, Fajardo, PR. ⓒ 866-317-8933 or 787-863-1000, ✆ 787-863-6758, 🖳 www.lascasitasvillage.com

💲 **Beyond Belief** 🍸 **CP** ⒸⒸ 155 rooms

Prices here start at around $800 a night for a one-bedroom villa *without* a water view, so we'd rather go to St. Barth—even if there *is* a personal butler who is assigned to each villa! There *are* limits. One of two "Five Diamond AAA Award" recipients in the Caribbean (the other is the Four Seasons on Nevis), Las Casitas offers one-, two-, and three-bedroom *casitas* and the Golden Door Spa. Designed to resemble a Spanish colonial village, the villas have a lot of the same amenities as their next-door neighbor, plus the aforementioned butler, 24-hour room service, private pool, fully equipped kitchen, and your favorite refreshments and reading materials stocked in your villa before you arrive. (No, they're not psychic, and they don't have access to your supermarket scanner card records. The reservations people ask lots of questions.) Needless to say, the villas are nicely done and quite luxurious. The villas are perched on a bluff that's 300 feet high, but you still have to take that damn water taxi to get to the beach! There are packages, but the rate category doesn't even come close to changing!

Naguabo and El Yunque Rainforest

Naguabo happens to be the closest town to the rainforest, although the town does not offer much to the visitor. Instead, we recommend driving to one of the inns listed below, which are located in the hills leading into El Yunque. Both places offer comfortable rooms with awe-inspiring views of the jungle. As we began twisting our way up the winding mountain roads, we understood why the Indians named Naguabo "the place where the mountains start." For camping enthusiasts, although there is no official campsite within the park, it is legal to pitch a tent. Simply stop at the National Forest's Palo Colorado Information Center (888-1810) on Road 191 any day before 4 p.m. to make a reservation.

Where to Stay

⊛ **Casa Flamboyant B&B**, P.O. Box 175, Naguabo, PR. ✆ 787-874-6074 or 787-613-3454, ✎ 787-874-6135, 🖳 www.rainforestsafari.com/flamboy.html,

💲 **Not So Cheap** 🍽 **BP** CC 4 rooms

Perched up in the mountains at the southern cusp of El Yunque Rainforest, this petite B&B sits on 25 lush and landscaped acres with more than 200 kinds of trees, 50 species of orchids, and at least 100 exotic ferns. Nearby waterfalls of the Cubuy River provide natural ambient sound. The tile deck of the small but attractive and heated swimming pool has distant views of the Caribbean to the southeast. Maybe that is why so many artists, from painters to ballet dancers, have spent so much time here. Even though this is a B&B, Chicago native Shirley has added artistic details and the amenities of luxury lodging, such as 350-thread-count sheets and a variety of massages. The eclectic décor runs from pink and frilly with painted angelic statuary to more sedate yellow tones and wood paneling. One guest room and the villa have terraces, and all rooms have private baths. We love the Rainbow Room with its own sitting room, complete with big art books. Casa Flamboyant is off the beaten path (roughly between Fajardo and Palmas de Mar) and thus a good choice for those seeking peace and quiet. Activities can be arranged, however. An easy hike down the hill leads to the natural pools at the river below. There are several local-style seafood restaurants in Playa Punta Santiago (about a 20-minute drive down the mountain). No children under 12 are allowed during the winter season.

Yunque Mar, Playa Fortuna, Luquillo, PR. ℂ 787-889-5555, ✆ 787-889-8048, 🖥 www.yunquemar.com, hotel@yunquemar.com

🍱 **Cheap** 🍴 **EP** ᴄᴄ 15 rooms

If you're wondering where the name of this hotel originated, imagine a cross between jungle and sea. Yes, this small hotel is ideally located between El Yunque Rainforest and the beautiful Luquillo Beach. It's also very close to Fajardo, making it a great location for those who are on their way to Vieques and Culebra. Standard rooms in this two-story white hotel overlooking the ocean have a/c and cable TV, but we recommend the upgrade to the sea view rooms, which have a balcony with great vistas. The beds are small — even the VIP suite has only a double bed — but the rooms are clean and airy. The price is right, especially considering the outrageous prices many pay for a sea view room here in Puerto Rico.

Casa Cubuy, P.O. Box 721, Rio Blanco, PR. ℂ 787-874-6221, 🖥 www.casacubuy.com, info@casacubuy.com

🍱 **Not So Cheap** 🍴 **BP** ᴄᴄ 10 rooms

We are always looking for hotels that allow us to live within the attraction. Instead of packing up and leaving our hotel in order to "see the sights," we prefer to have it all in our backyard. That is why we love Casa Cubuy, a small eco-lodge on the edge of El Yunque National Rainforest. Located high in the mountains, up a winding (paved) road from Naguabo, is this "healthy mountain retreat," which is run by ex-Floridian Marianne and her son, Matthew. Marianne has lived here since 1972, and in 1997 she decided to expand her house into a B&B. Each of the 10 rooms includes fans and huge sliding doors that open right onto the forest. Be sure to request one of the five upper-level rooms with spacious verandas over the forest. Those visitors arriving at night (like us) will be delighted to wake up to the unbelievable spread of green that greets them from their room. To sleep here is especially enjoyable — there are no mosquitoes at this altitude, and the quiet surroundings make sleeping a cinch. Best of all, the owners have built some leisurely trails that lead to the cascading river below. After an easy 10-minute walk, hikers are rewarded with a natural swimming pool in the crisp, clean river. There are also prehistoric rock carvings nearby — ask Matthew for more information. For those who are seeking more excitement, Marianne can arrange everything from massage to horseback riding. For sunny days, there is a sundeck; for rainy days — well, there is a library, and Wi-Fi is now available. There isn't a ton of style emanating from this inn, but the accommodations are quite comfortable and the staff is very helpful.

THE EAST COAST

Yabucoa

Yabucoa first earned its stripes as a cassava town but rose to prominence as Sugarcane City. There were once six sugar mills here, the most important being the granddaddy Central Riog that was in business for more than 70 years, closing in 1981. Today, Yabucoa draws people for its beaches, but with the exception of the *parador* listed below, there are hardly any dining options.

Where to Stay

Palmas de Lucia Parador, Roads 901 & 9911, Playa Lucía, Yabucoa, PR. ℂ 787-893-4423, 🖳 www.palmasdelucia.com, palmasdelucia@direcway.com

💲 **Cheap** 🍴 **BP** CC 34 rooms

For those who are craving more tranquillity and less fanfare than the over-the-top Sheraton, this local-owned *parador* is a pleasant option. The three-story hotel has its own pool and is steps from the Playa de Lucía, which gets crowded on weekends but is often quite desolate during the week. The rooms have sea views and either a king or two double beds and come equipped with TV, a/c, minibar, and microwave. The pool area includes a terrace with sun chairs, although we could do without the "Kodak Spot" sign that tells us this is a good photo spot (especially because the beach that's located just a few steps away is 10 times more picturesque). There is also a small restaurant and the always important basketball court for guests who need to work on their jump-shot. For a low-key beach experience at affordable prices, this *parador* doesn't offer much in terms of style, but it can be a pleasant getaway from the big resorts.

Costa del Mar Guest House, Carretera 901, km 5.6, Yabucoa, PR. ℂ 787-266-2868, ✎ 787-893-6374 🖳 www.costadelmargh.com, parador@palmasdelucia.com

💲 **Cheap** 🍴 **EP** CC 16 rooms

There are a few reasons we cannot give this guesthouse a ringing endorsement. First and foremost, we felt like Tantalus at this place. So close to the ocean, yet no beach access—it killed us! We learned that we had to go all the way to Palmas de Lucía Parador (same owners) just to swim. Sure, there is a pool here, but we crave the salty sea. This hotel is quite antiseptic, all the way down to the overwhelming aroma of cleaner we noticed upon first entry. The rooms are basic, with a/c, sliding glass door, and a tiny terrace without any furniture for enjoying the view. Since it's located out of the way, we

expected a restaurant, but there is no food offered. We found
it to be a bit of a pain to be forced to "hunt" for food in our
rental car.

Palmas del Mar

Located on the southeast coast near the town of Humacao on almost
2,800 acres, this is a condo-resort development of mammoth, sprawling, haphazard, and sometimes not-so-pretty proportions. Popular as
a weekend haven for Sanjuaneros (it's less than an hour from San
Juan) and snowbirds from North America, Palmas del Mar boasts
more than 3 miles of beaches (including one with lifeguards, bar,
and cafe); two 18-hole golf courses (designed by Gary Player and
Rees Jones); 20 tennis courts (7 lighted); an equestrian center; 7
pools; a fitness center; a large boat basin with several marinas and
Coral Head Divers; the rather stark and behemoth Palmanova Plaza
shopping center; more than 15 restaurants, cafes, and pizza joints;
several bars, and a casino. Sheraton has a resort here, and several of
the condo clusters have all kinds of rental units available. Although
we prefer other parts of Puerto Rico (Palmas is not our style), Palmas
del Mar might be a good and affordable alternative for families who
go the condo rental route. Contact Coldwell Banker or Diane Marsters
(800-835-0199 or 787-850-3030; www.marstersrealty.com), Palmas
del Mar Real Estate (787-852-8888), or RE/MAX de Palmas (787-850-
7069).

Where to Stay

Four Points Sheraton Palmas del Mar, 170 Candelero Drive,
    Humacao, PR. ✆ 787-850-6000, 🖷 787-850-6001,
    🖵 www.sheraton.com

💲 **Not So Cheap** 🍴 **EP** CC 107 rooms

We see this as more of a country club than a resort. Located
on a grandiose 2,750-acre resort, this Sheraton estate has recently been upgraded after a major renovation in 2004. We
aren't a big fan of the setup here, though; the hotel is located

in a sprawling subdevelopment that has an extremely non–Puerto Rican feel. With all the houses being built here, it seems that the hotel is a bit of an afterthought. The rooms are adequate and do have all the amenities, including Internet access, a private lanai, and the patented Sheraton Four Comfort Bed, which is extremely comfortable, if that is any consolation. The golf course is great for those who crave hitting the links. There is a heated infinity pool, a fitness center, a wine bar, and restaurants on site.

THE SOUTH COAST

Patillas

On our most recent visit to Puerto Rico, we discovered this relaxed minicity, which retains an authentic small-town Puerto Rican feel. Patillas was named after the watermelon, but its claim to fame is the juicy grapes that are harvested here and sold to American winemakers. Patillas is also called "The Emerald of the South"—one look at the sparkling water of the beaches will explain why. Patillas is the perfect place to relax and kick back—especially if, like us, you spent too much time in the clubs while visiting San Juan.

Where to Stay

Caribe Playa Beach Resort, HC 764, P.O. Box 8490, Patillas, PR. ✆ 787-839-6339, ✎ 787-839-1817, 🖳 www.caribeplaya.com, luisnazario@caribeplaya.com

🛍 **Not So Cheap** 🍴 **EP** CC 29 rooms

Tucked within a secluded cove on the southeastern coast is this little gem. Sure, nobody has ever heard of Patillas, but that is half the fun. This is where the rainforest descends to the crescent-shaped beach, which is testimony to the natural beauty of this less-traveled corner of Puerto Rico. If you're looking for the comfort of a resort without the extravagance (or stratospheric prices), this unassuming hotel is the perfect option. This family-run establishment has recently come under a new management that is intent on catering to its guests' every need.

The hotel is an ochre and white two-story structure, and each of the rooms has direct sea views. Unlike at some resorts that are built way off the shore, the balconies here are right over the beach — a private beach, at that, complete with sun chairs to soak up the Puerto Rican sun. There is also a sundeck, a relaxing pool area, a barbecue grill, and hammocks. The grounds are nicely landscaped with plenty of palms and plants. The stretch of beach here is beautiful, with tall palms hanging right over the sea. Each room, though not stylish, has either two double beds or a queen and includes a/c, fan, cable TV, minibar, phone, and coffeemaker. There is also Internet access, a library, and a TV room for those non-nature types. The restaurant has recently switched over to Latino-Caribbean fusion cuisine and has done a fine job in the process.

It's no surprise that many of the resort's clientele are repeat guests — after our stay, we were aching to return, too. Sure, the hotel is not located in one of the island's main tourist zones, but that is a blessing, not a curse. Right in front of the beach, there is surfing, swimming, and snorkeling (dolphin and manta rays are commonly sighted), so be sure to bring your snorkel gear. The picturesque town of Patillas is just five minutes by foot, providing an authentic glimpse of the real Puerto Rico — more than any super-resort will ever offer.

Caribbean Paradise Parador, Road 3, km 114, Barrio Guadarraya, Patillas, PR. ✆ 787-839-5885 or -7388, ✉ 787-271-0069, 🖥 www.caribbeanparadisepr.com, caribbean@isla.net

🚫 Cheap 🍴 EP CC 23 rooms

For a 10-year-old who doesn't like the beach, this hotel may be a "Caribbean Paradise," but for us, it's a nightmare. First of all, it's not on the beach, which causes it to automatically lose its "paradise" tag. It's only about a block and a half off the shore, but it gets quite hot without the sea breeze. The hotel has little to brag about except the array of video games and playground equipment for toddlers. The rooms have a/c, coffeemaker, and cable TV but are boxy. The rooms have no fans, so it's uncomfortable to keep the windows open, making for a bit of a claustrophobic experience. There are two pools, one of which is designated for kids. We are starting to think that this hotel was opened by kids, as they seem to enjoy all the amenities. This place has no flair or local flavor — just a lot of kids' toys.

Ponce

Known as "The Pearl of the South," Ponce is a wonderful mélange of Spanish and Caribbean architecture, with other styles thrown in for the hell of it. The city was founded by Ponce de León's great-grandson, who proceeded to name it after, who else, his great-granddaddy. In downtown Ponce, the Spanish colonial influence is still very pronounced. Most of the central district around **Plaza Las Delicias** has been or is in the process of being restored and is definitely worth seeing. In the plaza are the **Catedral Nuestra Señora de Guadalupe** and the very colorful old firehouse, the **Parque de Bombas**, which sparkles after its recent renovation. Other must-stops while in Ponce are the **Museo de la Música Puertorriqueña**, (848-7016, at the corner of Calles Isabel and Salud and open Tuesday through Sunday, 8:30 a.m. to 4:30 p.m.), which provides a great perspective on Puerto Rican music from *bomba* and *plena* to *danza* and *salsa*; the neoclassical and colorful facade of **Teatro La Perla** (Calle Mayor); the **Museum of the History of Ponce** (Casa Salazar), 844-7071, open every day except Tuesday from 9 a.m. to 5 p.m., admission $3 for adults and $1.50 for children; and the world-class **Ponce Museum of Art**, 848-0505, open daily from 10 a.m. to 5 p.m., admission $4 for adults and $2 for children. Note that once you leave the center of town, there are very few street signs, so be sure to have a good map and a sense of humor.

Just south of town, past the Ponce Hilton at the end of Route 14 (Avenida Malecón), is **La Guancha Paseo Tablado**, a happening boardwalk on the water that is lined with bars, cafes, and restaurants. It's a hangout spot for both young and old Ponceños. We like having a cold Medalla or piña colada and watching the crowd, boats (it's a marina, too), and water. The trade winds keep things cool. There is also a pier where you can catch a boat to **Caja de Muertos** (Coffin Island). On the island there is a gorgeous beach for swimming, excellent snorkeling, and an old lighthouse built in 1880. **Aventuras Puerto Rico** (380-8481) leads trips here and all over Puerto Rico.

Where to Stay

Hotel Meliá, P.O. Box 1431, 75 Calle Cristina, Ponce, PR.
   © 800-448-8355 or 787-842-0260, ✆ 787-841-3602,
   🖳 www.hotelmeliapr.com, info@hotelmeliapr.com

   💲 **Cheap** and up 🍴 **EP** CC 73 rooms

   Located adjacent to the Parque de Bombas, this family-owned and -operated hotel has no relation to the Spanish giant Meliá Hotels chain. Rather, it is a very affordable hotel that sits within walking distance of all the historic sites of central Ponce. The clean, simple (and somewhat retro-funky) rooms all include a/c, private bath, phone, and cable TV. The rooms on the high floors offer some nice views, especially those facing west and the Plaza Las Delicias. There is a wonderful rooftop terrace where breakfast is served — it is also a great place for evening cocktails. The recent completion of a swimming pool has elevated the Meliá above the competition. There is a restaurant and bar at the hotel, and you are steps away from countless others. We loved the lobby's Spanish charm — tile floors, high ceilings, faded décor — and the last time we visited, there were plastic covers on the lampshades (so antichic!). A newly added Executive Center (a room with two computers) offers free Wi-Fi Internet access for guests.

Hilton Ponce Golf & Casino Resort, P.O. Box 7419, 1150 Avenida Caribe, Ponce, PR. © 800-HILTONS or 787-259-7676,
   ✆ 787-259-7674, 🖳 www.hilton.com

   💲 **Very Pricey** and up 🍴 **EP** CC 253 rooms

Geared to the business traveler, the blue and white Ponce Hilton is the city's biggest hotel and the largest resort on Puerto Rico's south coast. Located about 10 minutes south of the Plaza Las Delicias (depending on traffic), this hotel is lacking in warmth and charm. Indeed, the lobby has the feel of a suburban mall. The property has 80 acres, is on the waterfront (although the beach in front is not very pretty), and sea views are decent only from the top (fourth) floor. It does have a putting green and driving range, four lighted tennis courts, a pool, a fitness center, a basketball court, a playground, and a pool table (we love eight-ball). There are seven restaurants and bars (including the Pavilion Discotheque), and, of course, the casino. The rooms, furnished in rattan and tropical colors, are loaded with amenities, including a/c, lanai, cable TV with video games, Internet access, speakerphone with voicemail and data port, safe, minibar, and iron and ironing board. Look for packages or corporate discounts.

Hotel Belgica, 122-C Villa, Ponce, PR. ℰ and ✆ 787-844-3255, 🖥 www.hotelbelgica.com, hotelbelgica@yahoo.com

🟥$ **Cheap** 🍽 **EP** ⓒⓒ 20 rooms

The cheapest of the three hotels located in the heart of Ponce is this old-fashioned spot. Right off the plaza, the Belgica offers easy access to the city and features rooms with high ceilings, comfortable beds, and Spanish-style balconies. The sheets are a bit starched and the towels not much softer than sandpaper, but the rates are cheap and the rooms pleasant. For those who don't mind street noise, the rooms with a balcony are recommended. There is no restaurant, pool, or other amenities of that sort.

Fox Delicias Hotel, 6963 Calle Isabel, Ponce, PR. ℰ 787-290-5050, ✆ 787-290-5005, 🖥 www.foxdeliciashotel.com

🟥$ **Not So Cheap** 🍽 **EP** ⓒⓒ 30 rooms

Hey, all you mall lovers, we have found your paradise! The Fox Delicias bills itself as "your downtown getaway," but we have deemed it "the mall rat's Eden." What was once Ponce's mall has recently been converted to a hotel and, best of all, it has retained the feel of a shopping mall! Upon entering, we couldn't help but notice that the layout has remained the same. What were once small shops have been equipped with beds and bathrooms, and even the beauty salon has survived the makeover (excuse the pun). This place is so tacky that we found ourselves running for the exits! We are not mall haters, but who would build a hotel with 30 rooms without windows? Excuse us, *only* 28 of the 30 are self-enclosed. It's great for those who have always fantasized about staying in the mall after closing time, but it's a nightmare for those of us who like a little fresh air or at least a window to remind us that we aren't in prison. Sure, the rooms have cable TV, a/c, and a phone, but the ceilings are low and the atmosphere is as stuffy as a tiny gift shop (coincidence?). The mall's escalators remain, although the kiosk with the "You are here" sign has mercifully been dismantled. Can we use the word *tacky* again? The owners have even held on to that mall mainstay, the food court. Guests emerge from their windowless rooms on the ground floor to be greeted by a slew of people seated right in front of their door, chowing down on one of the five cheap daily specials. High class it's not. For those searching for the sleep-in-the-mall experience, call the number above. If not, steer clear of the Fox Mall, err... we mean, Hotel.

Where to Eat

$$$ **El Ancla**, 805 Avenida Hostos, 840-2450
We love sitting at this seaside restaurant, where the waves caress the shore as we dine on great *criollo* cuisine, such as the famous seafood stew. El Ancla is located on the docks just south of the city. It's very popular, so directions are easy to come by. Open 11:30 a.m. to 9:30 p.m. and later on weekends.

$$$$ **La Terraza**, in Ponce Hilton, 1150 Avenida Caribe, 259-7676
Although housed in a big hotel, La Terraza has an ambiance that is quite conducive to a great dining experience. The colonial décor and New World charm, coupled with the acclaimed

cuisine, keep tourists and locals coming back for more. The menu changes every few months, but expect Caribbean specialties with a creative flair and excellent presentation. Open for dinner from 6 to 10 p.m. Reservations recommended.

$$ **Lupita's Mexican Restaurant**, 60 Calle Isabel, off the plaza, 812-4499
This is as close to bona fide Mexican food as we have found here in Puerto Rico. The open courtyard, decorated in authentic Mexican tile work, is a great place to sample the chimichangas, fajitas, or whatever Mexican delicacy you crave. The margaritas are spot-on. Open 11 a.m. to 11 p.m.

$$$ **Pito's Seafood**, Road 2, 841-4977
This is one of our favorite seafood spots. It offers three floors of open-air seaside dining. Pito's has its fancy side, such as its wine cellar, but the mood here is casual and comfortable. Seafood abounds—dig in. It also has a "Wine Oysters Espresso" Bar, but we urge readers not to mix all three in the same glass. With live music on the weekends and endless ocean breezes, Pito's is a great spot from which to enjoy the scenery. Open from 11 a.m. to 11 p.m. Sunday through Thursday; Friday and Saturday until midnight.

Guánica and La Parguera

Located on the southern coast of the island, west of Ponce and near three great natural sites—the Guánica Forest Reserve, the Phosphorescent Bay, and Gilligan's Island—Guánica is an example of the "real" Puerto Rico. There are few fast-food chains, 7-Elevens, or Blockbuster Videos—just lots of *bodegas* and *panaderías*. Guánica has a cool-looking waterfront (camera, please), and just outside town, the **Guánica Forest Reserve** has some gorgeous and deserted beaches. To get to the Reserve, just follow Route 333 until you can go no farther. You'll see places to stop along the way. Guánica also has some of the best dive sites in Puerto Rico. **Gilligan's Island** is a small, uninhabited, mile-offshore cay with a secluded beach and excellent snorkeling. The folks at Copamarina, 821-0505, can arrange an excursion there.

About 10 miles west of Guánica is La Parguera and **Phosphorescent Bay** (Route 324—watch for signs). La Parguera is a fishing town with a handful of restaurants and a few bars where we like to play pool with the locals. Most go there for the "bio bay," as it's called—in the dark of a calm night, phosphorescent plankton (dinoflagellates, to be precise) create sparks when there's any movement in the water, which disturbs their nesting. La Parguera's coastline is filled with mangrove islands and is not a beach destination. However, the harbor is a haven for fishing charters, especially the deep-sea variety. Call **Parguera Fishing Charters** (787-899-4698) for more info. **Aleli Tours** (390-6086) runs sailing, snorkeling, and kayaking tours. Its catamaran is available for charter. Our favorite dive shop in town is **Paradise Scuba** (899-7611), which leads dives to the bioluminescent bay.

Where to Stay

Copamarina Beach Resort, P.O. Box 805, Route 333, km 6.5, Caña
  Gorda, Guánica, PR. ✆ 800-468-4553 or 787-821-0505,
  ✉ 787-821-0070, 💻 www.copamarina.com,
  info@copamarina.com

💲 **Pricey** and up 🍴 **EP** CC 106 rooms

  Copamarina is a reasonably priced resort situated on the Bahía de Guánica in a quiet part of the island. It has recently expanded and now has 106 rooms and suites spread out over 16 acres. The rooms are attractive—with wall-to-wall carpeting or tile floors, bamboo and light wood furnishings, a/c, cable TV, fridges, safes, hairdryers, coffeemakers, and phones— and they sport little lanais. The main lobby has a very pleasant veranda on which to sit and read.

  This is a great place to go if you want to be somewhere tranquil and be near the extensive Guánica Forest Reserve (where you can take long walks or bike rides). Copamarina is very popular with weekenders from San Juan who want a secluded getaway. The grounds are well tended and the beach is pretty. The seas here are calm because the bay is sheltered. However, sometimes after storms, the water contains lots of seaweed. (If only we could control the weather.) There are more beaches close by in the Forest Reserve. The beach area here has recently been spruced up and embellished by big raised beds that are ideal for relaxing in the sun, sipping piña coladas, or sunbathing topless. There are two pools, a kids' pool, full water sports—including a full-service PADI Dive Center—a small fitness center, and two lighted tennis courts. For dining, there is the open-air Las Palmas Café and the new Alexandra Restaurant, which offers gourmet Caribbean dining in an elegant dining room or out on the terrace and has a live guitarist most nights.

Parador Guánica 1929, Avenida Los Veteranos, km 2.5 & Road 3116, Guánica, PR. ✆ 787-821-0099, ✉ 787-821-1842, 🖳 www.guanica1929.com, parador@palmasdelucia.com

💲 **Cheap** 🍴 **EP** or **All-Inclusive** ⓒⓒ 27 rooms

Back in the days when this region was prime sugar-growing territory, there were lots of investors, "sugar daddies," and bigwigs passing through these parts. In 1929, the stately Hotel Americano was built on this site to accommodate these important guests. Today the sugar industry is no longer king, but thankfully this historic hotel has recently been re-opened. With experience running *paradores,* Juan and Maria have done a fine job here as well. They have completely renovated the property and have geared it toward families, Puerto Rican and foreign alike, who are looking for an affordable vacation spot. The rooms within the peach-colored, two-story hotel include verandas with views of Ensenada Bay. Below is an appealing pool area with sun chairs. It offers an all-inclusive plan that is quite affordable—the food from the à la carte *criollo* restaurant is good, but we like the freedom to try new spots in town or at the Copamarina. Legend has it that Teddy Roosevelt stayed here, but we don't think he had a/c or cable TV, as we did. A note to drinkers: Due to a family-friendly policy, no alcohol is served at the Guánica.

Parador Villa Parguera, Carretera 304, km 3.3, Lajas, PR. ✆ 787-899-7777, ✉ 787-899-6040, 🖳 www.villaparguera.net, pvparguera@aol.com

💲 **Not So Cheap** 🍴 **EP** CC 74 rooms

Perched right on the seafront in downtown La Parguera, this three-story hotel is not overflowing with style, by any means, but the rooms are well equipped, clean, and affordable. Each has cable TV and a/c but no fan. One reason we prefer staying in the aforementioned Guánica is that there is no beach here, to speak of (although sun chairs are set out on the grass along the rocky sea front). The swinging palms provide some shade, and there is a small pool. The on-site restaurant is a bit bleak —hardly the *Méson Gastronomico* it's billed to be. On weekends, the hotel puts on small-scale floor shows. The dock for the bioluminescent bay trips is located just a few steps away —quite convenient if you're up for a nighttime algae show.

THE WEST COAST

Boquerón

Located in an area called Cabo Rojo in the southwestern corner of the island, Boquerón used to be a charming little village, but over the past decade it has grown tremendously. Boquerón has a beautiful long beach and calm bay and is considered one of Puerto Rico's best bathing beaches. For this reason, it has become a very popular weekend getaway spot for Sanjuaneros (just over a two-hour drive). The bay is very scenic, with mountains at the southern end. Actually, the entire area is quite wonderful. It's rural, with pastures and herds of cattle reaching up to green hills and mountains.

It's also a boat town —lots of cruising boats stop here, bringing with them those weathered and boozy "boat rats." Now, we're not one to bitch about a few cocktails. After all, Nick and Nora Charles (and, of course, Patsy Stone) are our idols. But these people start early, hang out at the bar for hours, get totally blotto, and by a miracle of gravitation and balance, somehow manage to get back to their boats intact. They're always in their berths early because they get so trashed. We're amused as long as they don't start talking to us in an advanced state of inebriation. If they do, we excuse ourselves to go to the loo and never return.

The center of activity in Boquerón is the main intersection in town, by the bay, where there are two prominent bars on opposite corners. The one with the action and a very competitive pool table is called **Shamar**. You know it's a yachty favorite from all the tattered burgees and ensigns donated to the bar by boaters from yacht clubs and countries around the world. Although this place used to get quite rowdy on weekends, recent ordinances have put an end to the mayhem. Weekend nights are still fun—the streets are blocked off and the town bustles with a young crowd. The public beach is great, but if you're aching to get off the beaten track, check out Playa Buyó, which is about 2 miles north of town. **Mona Aquatics** (851-2185) has a full range of activities, from scuba to snorkeling in bio bay—it is right next to the marina. We also recommend renting kayaks to explore the waters here—**Boquerón Kayak Rental** (255-1849) can arrange everything. We have listed our favorite hotels, but for those looking for apartment rentals, contact **Centro Vacacional Boquerón** at 787-851-1900; it has access to more than 150 beachside apartments with kitchens (although many apartments have those often-annoying bunk beds).

Where to Stay

Parador Boquemar, P.O. Box 133, Route 101, Boquerón, Cabo Rojo, PR. ✆ 787-851-2158, ✉ 787-851-7600, 🖥 www.boquemar.com, reservacion@boquemar.com

🛒 Cheap 🍴 EP CC 75 rooms

This pink *parador* in Boquerón resembles a motel but is clean, efficient, and cheap. Recently renovated, this three-story hotel's rooms are equipped with a/c, fridge, phone, cable TV, and private bath. There is a swimming pool, a restaurant (La Cascada), and a bar. The rooms on the second and third floors have lanais. The town junction (where all the activity happens) and the beach are just around the corner and down the street. Be sure to make reservations well in advance—the

Boquemar is popular with folks from San Juan on weekends. It's not glamorous, but it's more modern than many *paradores*.

Cofresí Beach Hotel, 57 Calle Munoz Rivera, Boquerón, Cabo Rojo, PR. ✆ 787-254-3000, ✎ 787-254-1048, 🖥 www.cofresibeach.com

💰 **Not So Cheap** 🍴 EP Ⓒⓒ 12 apartments

This art deco–like hotel offers one-, two-, and three-bedroom apartments, all of which are equipped with fully functioning kitchens. The bedrooms include queen-size beds, a/c, and dial-up Internet access (good luck with that). For television buffs, each apartment includes cable TV and a DVD player. The hotel also has a small rectangular pool and views of the sea. The beach is a hop, skip, and a jump away, and the prices are reasonable. It's a good option for the simple traveler craving a cheap spot close to the action and the beach.

Boquerón Beach Hotel, Boquerón, Cabo Rojo, PR. ✆ and ✎ 787-851-7110, 🖥 www.boqueronbeachhotel.com

💰 **Cheap** 🍴 EP Ⓒⓒ 88 rooms

Though not right in town, this older hotel is blessed with original Spanish tile work and colonial-style wrought-iron balconies. Recent renovations have also given some of the rooms a well-needed sprucing up. The rooms have TV, a/c, and mini-bar. Request one of the rooms in front—these are the best. For those who don't mind being right out of town, this quiet old hotel is a good bet. It is located by the entrance to the public beach (Balneario de Boquerón). There is a pool but no restaurant.

Where to Eat

In Boquerón, there are options within town and on the outlying beaches. Of the restaurants in town, our favorites are listed below. In the morning, there are several little cheap and simple breakfast spots next to the happening bars. Some of the nearby beaches are ideal for a visit and a seaside meal. This is perhaps the best place on the island to sample the fresh oysters and clams. They are available along Calle de Diego (the beach road) from vendors who crack them open upon demand. **El Combate** is one of the best beaches in the region, and most of the nearby restaurants are quite similar, so make a visit and take a look around. Just up the coast, **Joyuda** is known for its seafood and has several good restaurants, including **Perichi's** (851-3131), **Tino's** (851-2976), and **Annie's** (851-0021), which has the best food.

$$$ **El Bohío**, Carretera 102, km 13.9, Joyuda, 851-2755
This is our favorite restaurant here. We love to sit on the deck over the water. The menu is Caribbean and seafood—the cold conch salad is a perfect light lunch option.

$$$ **Fishnet**, Calle José de Diego, 254-3163
It is only fitting that this centrally located restaurant has a marine theme, because Boquerón's best seafood is cooked here. The owner has another restaurant a few steps away called **Roberto's Villa Playera**, which has the same quality food with better views. Either one is a solid bet for fresh fish and more.

$$$ **Galloway's**, 12 Calle José de Diego, 254-3302
We love the location, perched above the sea. Beautiful sunsets (and of course, happy-hour specials) make this a popular hangout spot. The food is well prepared, with a focus on seafood and pasta. All the seafood is extremely fresh. Daily lunch specials are quite affordable, and the American owners, Dan and Gladys, are good conversationalists as well.

$$$ **Pika-Pika**, 244 Calle Estacion, 851-2440
Though a little pricey, this Mexican restaurant warrants a few extra bucks. Its specialties are meat plates, served with all the fixings. It has a varied cocktail menu and offers weekend lunches.

$$ **Pizzeria Lykken**, Calle José de Diego, 851-6335
For the best pizza around, Lykken is the way to go. We like the outdoor terrace and the big selection of pies. Open until 10 p.m.

Going Out

Galloway's is a popular spot for drinks, catering to the Irish pub crowd. Rock music predominates. However, most of the action centers around **Shamar** (851-0542), which has happy-hour specials, pool tables, and a lively atmosphere. Beers are cheap, and live bands play salsa music on the weekend.

Mayagüez

After San Juan and Ponce, this is Puerto Rico's largest city. Mayagüez is one of the island's major ports, but it is hardly a metropolis. Much of the city was destroyed in an earthquake in 1918, but the central square, **Plaza Colón**, is attractive, as is the City Hall that flanks it. **Teatro Yagüez** has a lot of history and now stands as the cultural nexus for western Puerto Rico. Mayagüez is also the site of the island's major university and zoo, which has been recently renovated to provide more living space for the animals.

Where to Stay

Mayagüez Resort & Casino, Route 104, km. 0.3, Mayagüez, PR.
Ⓒ 787-832-3030, ✎ 787-265-3020,
💻 www.mayaguezresort.com
💲 **Very Pricey** 🍴 **All-Inclusive** ⒸⒸ 140 rooms

Fifteen minutes out of Mayagüez, this hilltop resort is set on 25 acres and offers beautiful bay views. The problem is that it's not much of a resort. Sure, there is a pool, a few tennis courts, and a small gym, but besides that there is not much offered. The rooms, which are housed in a five-story boxy building overlooking a nonspectacular pool, have a/c and cable TV. The hotel does offer free Wi-Fi throughout the hotel, 24-hour room service, and a big casino that is a popular hangout. There are restaurants on site and a pool bar as well. We do like the tropical grounds here — there are beautiful trees and flowers, but it seems that everyone else was too busy tossing quarters into the slot machines to notice.

Howard Johnson Mayagüez, 70 Calle Mendez Vigo, Mayagüez, PR.
© 800-446-4656 or 787-832-9191, *✆* 787-832-9122,
💻 www.hojo.com, veleztom1@wynhg.com

💲 **Not So Cheap** *🍴* **EP** **CC** 39 rooms

This brand-new member of the once illustrious Howard Johnson hotel chain has at least a tad of local flavor — it was built in the town's old convent. We find it kind of strange to stay in a penthouse in the nuns' house, but for those seeking layman luxury, there are four of these top-floor suites. In addition to having free Wi-Fi, each of the rooms has exactly what one would expect from HoJo's — cable TV, a/c, hairdryer, iron and ironing board, coffeemaker, and tacky comforters. There is a teeny-weeny pool in the enclosed courtyard — apparently the sisters were not big pool-goers. Located right in the heart of town, HoJo's is a good spot from which to tour the city or act out any converted convent fantasies.

Hotel Colonial, 14 Calle Iglesia Sur, Mayagüez, PR. *©* and
✆ 787-833-2150, *💻* www.hotelcolonial.com, colonial@
hotel-colonial.com

💲 **Cheap** *🍴* **CP** **CC** 29 rooms

This old-fashioned hotel has been lodging visitors for at least 90 years — that's a lot of dirty sheets! Not surprisingly, the Colonial is a little aged. The original ceramic floor tiles are still found in some rooms, which is a welcome bridge to the past, but the tacky furniture within brings back memories of the late 1970s — which was a great era for disco parties, but not for hotel furnishings. There are not enough windows for our liking, either — many rooms do not have any at all. The rooms have free DSL Internet access, a/c, cable TV, a minibar, and, although there are new mattresses on every bed, not much in the style department. There is no restaurant, pool, or fitness room.

Where to Eat and Go Out

$$ **El Castillo,** in Mayagüez Resort, Route 104, 832-3030
This is the best place in town for a hearty meal. The lunch

buffet on weekdays is chock full of local dishes — a great opportunity to sample everything under the Puerto Rican sun.
The breakfast buffet is plentiful, although it is usually devoured
by the hotel guests. The weekend brunch is, well, a combination of the two, which makes sense. Dinners are à la carte
— we recommend the sea bass. Open 6:30 a.m. to midnight.

$$$ **Restaurant El Estoril**, 100 E. Calle Mendez Vigo, 834-2288
By far the best restaurant in town, El Estoril offers a wonder-
ful selection of sophisticated fare. The appetizers, such as es-
cargot, seviche, and Galician soup, are fantastic, and the en-
trées are no disappointment, either. The fish is served in a
variety of ways: with capers, port sauce, or, our favorite, creole
sauce. The scallop-stuffed crepes are also worth a try. Open
Monday through Saturday from 5:30 to 10:30 p.m.

Note that the bar next door, **La Galeria**, is a great place to
get a drink and enjoy jazz and blues music. It opens after 10
p.m. every day (although it's closed on Sunday) and usually
has live bands on the weekend. There is also a popular sports
bar, **Red Corner** (313-6943), also on Calle Mendez Vigo, that
has plenty of action.

Rincón

This corner of Puerto Rico is a surfer's mecca. Actually, some of the
best surfing in the Caribbean is found here during the winter
months. There are more than 20 surf spots in the Rincón-Aguadilla
area, with names like Dogman's, Domes, and Shithouse, and several
surf shops. A visit to the local post office will turn up as many
bleached-out surfer dudes as Puerto Ricans. Rincón is also one of the
most anglicized parts of the island. Being on the west coast, sunsets
are fantastic, whether viewed from a beachside bar, hotel balcony, or
the ocean surf. During the winter months (January until March) the
whales migrate to Rincón — they are visible from the lighthouse park
or from private boats available for excursions. **Punta Higuero** is
where the lighthouse stands — north of the lighthouse are the best
surf spots and popular hangouts; to the south are deserted beaches

such as the beautiful Playa Córcega. Pick up a copy of the tourist map for $1 at many locations or visit the **Tourist Information Center** (787-823-5024) at the intersection of Routes 413 and 115. A rental car is a must if you stay in the area. There is an airport in Aguadilla (about a 30-minute drive). Most people fly into San Juan (about 95 miles away and more than a two-hour drive). **West Coast Surf Shop** is right in downtown Rincón (823-3935). It rents out boogie and surf boards for $15 a day (weekly rates are also available). There are other nearby surf shops that rent out boards — try **Desecho Inn Surf Shop** near the lighthouse (823-0390).

Taino Divers (823-6429) is the most reputable dive shop in Rincón, specializing in two-tank dive trips to Desecho Island. There is often 100-foot visibility, and the wealth of marine life is astounding. U.S. Coast Guard Captain Tim runs **Cactus Fishing Charters** (833-0308), which offers great full-day trips. **Oceans Unlimited** (823-2340) charters boats from Puerto Real to Mona Island and beyond.

Where to Stay

⊛ **The Horned Dorset Primavera**, P.O. Box 1132, Route 429, km 3.0, Rincón, PR. ℂ 800-633-1857 or 787-823-4030, ✆ 787-823-5580, 🖳 www.horneddorset.com, info@horneddorset.com

🔓 **Ridiculous** ⑨ **EP** and **MAP** ⒸⒸ 22 suites; 17 private villas to come

Fine food, tranquillity, and service seem to be the mantra here at this sophisticated inn. Cheers to that! We love the Horned Dorset Primavera, a small and lovely 4-acre property, tucked away on the coast south of Rincón (so tucked away that we have driven by it on two separate occasions). It's a symphony of taste with a touch of attitude (the management still requests that guests refrain from cell phone use in the lobby), and owners Harold Davies, Wilhelm Sack, and Kingsley Wratten have gone to great pains to make the property a tranquil and comfortable hideaway. Named after Davies and Wratten's first inn in upstate New York, it is well appointed, nicely decorated, has a very attractive staff, and features a fantastic library. Readers will be thrilled. You can sink into a big comfy chair, order a drink, check out the spectacular western view of the water (or the staff), and occasionally look up to see who might be passing through the lobby—a piece of heaven to some, including us. Breakfast is served on the veranda of the main building or in your room (we had it on our lanai in our bathrobes—it is a great touch). Lunch is on the veranda or by the main pool. The hotel's prix fixe dining room, which we found a tad stuffy, features delicious French cuisine with Caribbean accents by chef Aaron Wratten. There is also a casual bistro, a fully equipped gym, and massage services. The hotel can arrange activities such as tennis, horseback riding, and diving.

In keeping with the tone of the property, the recently renovated 22 two-story suites still do not have TVs or radios, but phones have been added. These suites are extremely stylish, comfortable, and tasteful, with four-poster mahogany king-size beds and antiques. They also have lanais with a full or partial ocean view, a/c, and a ceiling fan. Some have private plunge pools. The very large bathrooms have brass claw-foot tubs, large vanities and mirrors (we love that—room for everyone's toiletries), and lots of white marble.

As if it were possible, this elegant inn is being upgraded to "become the most exclusive beachfront property on the island," according to Sack. In addition to the recent enhancements to the 22 suites, there are 17 new villas that are in the works for completion by the fall of 2007. These villas will (unfortunately, in our opinion) become super-exclusive condos that will be selling in the million-dollar-plus range. Each residence will retain the Horned Dorset's Mozarabic style and will include a private dipping pool and ocean view. The interiors will be ultra-fancy, with marble floors, oversize tubs, Kohler surround showers, plasma TV with DVD, Wi-Fi Internet access, wine cooler, and a fully equipped Dwyer kitchen. Although the units will be sold as condos, many will still be rented out to visitors—at least that's the plan. Nobody can be sure how participatory the individual condo owners will be when it comes to renting out their villas. Either way, we do hope that this new condo conversion will not spoil the special ambiance of the Horned Dorset. If the currently discussed plan for an on-site heliport is any indication, the days of no cell phone use in the lobby will be long gone.

That being said, we won't argue with the expected arrival of valet parking and spa services (who would complain about a spa?). Rounding out the amenities on the well-manicured grounds are a medium-size pool, a smaller pool on the top of the hill by the Mesa Suites, and a tiny beach for sunning and swimming. However, we'd say the main reason to come here (at least, for now) is to read, be quiet, spend time with your companion, and enjoy great food, or maybe have that secret tryst with that certain someone. The hotel does not have facilities for children, and no one under 12 is accepted as a guest. We say hooray for the HDP! No crying babies, strollers, or whining kids to distract us from the latest Danielle Steele novel.

We recommend the MAP upgrade for an additional $160 per couple per day.

⊛ **Casa Isleña Inn,** P.O. Box 1484, Road 413, km 4.8, Barrio Puntas, Rincón, PR. ✆ 888-289-7750 or 787-823-1525, ✉ 787-823-1530, 🖥 www.casa-islena.com, reservations@casa-islena.com

💲 **Not So Cheap** 🍴 **CP** ⓒⓒ 9 rooms

Ah, this is the life! That's how we would sum up our experience at the Casa Isleña, our one of our favorite spots in Rincón. It's not nearly as sophisticated as the Horned Dorset, but it's the ideal beach house. Located smack dab on the beautiful beach, close to the action, this sexy Mediterranean-style house has just nine rooms, which limits the number of guests. In 2002, Colombian owner Dario renovated what was a private residence into this beachfront inn, injecting his easygoing style and friendly nature. Vibrant colors run throughout. Regardless of the season, the inn is usually full, which comes as no surprise to us. Each of the rooms has one or two queen-size beds as well as a fan, a/c, cable TV, and terra-cotta floors.

The Mexican tiles and well-crafted handmade wooden furniture (also imported from Mexico) add a stylistic flair. We prefer the upstairs rooms with a view, especially Room 254, which has a king-size bed and a Jacuzzi in the bathroom. The small on-site restaurant serves fresh foods, such as salads and seafood. With a limited number of guests and an attractive beachside pool, the Casa Isleña maintains a friendly atmosphere and is a perfect choice, especially considering how much less expensive it is to stay here than at the Horned Dorsett.

Lemontree Waterfront Cottages, P.O. Box 200, Route 429, Rincón, PR. ✆ 888-418-8733 or 787-823-6452, ✉ 787-823-5821, 🖥 www.lemontreepr.com, info@lemontreepr.com

💰 **Not So Cheap** and up 🍴 **EP** **CC** 6 suites

Just down the road from the ultra-fancy Horned Dorset is this sort of funky place. Located so close to the water that a misstep will virtually put you in the drink, the Lemontree is two houses linked together by a patio. The property has a seawall, steps down to the water, and a sliver of sand (and we mean *sliver*). Owned and operated by Lov and Lora Carabello, there are six efficiency units—two studios, two one-bedroom cottages, one two-bedroom apartment, and one three-bedroom apartment. All have simple rattan furnishings, some custom woodwork, lanais that face west and toward the Mona Passage (we love the views), fully equipped kitchens (with blender, coffeemaker, and microwave), tile floors, flat-screen cable TV with DVD, Wi-Fi, a/c, and ceiling fans. The three-bedroom Papaya unit has a wet bar on the lanai. Maid service and linen change occurs halfway through your stay. Laundry service is available for a small fee. There is no pool or restaurant, but that is no problem given its beachside location and the presence of full kitchens in the suites. There is a three-night minimum.

Pipon's Resort, P.O. Box 4468, HC-01, Route 413, km 3, Barrio Puntas, Rincón, PR. ✆ 787-823-7154 or -5106, ✉ 787-823-6748, 🖥 www.piponsresort.com, sales@piponsresort.com

💰 **Not So Cheap** 🍴 **EP** **CC** 6 apartments

Run by Harry and Marthy, a friendly Puerto Rican–New Jersey couple, Pipon's is an ideal option for those travelers seeking more tranquillity and/or a chance to cook their own food. Think of it as a sea-view apartment with daily maid service. All apartments are clean and modern and have a/c, ceiling fans, and a fully stocked kitchen that includes a full stove and refrigerator. There is a bedroom with a queen-size bed as well as a sitting room with wicker cushioned furniture and cable TV. Our favorite feature, however, is the large private lanai, with its expansive and refreshing sea views. (The beach is 1,000 feet away, and accessed by a newly laid path.) An adequate pool with a sundeck sits just below the rooms. Pipon's is a perfect spot for those who want to get away from the typical resort experience. Its homey setting is great for families —cots and cribs are available upon request. Since there are not many culinary options around Rincón, access to a kitchen is quite a plus.

(★) **Rincón of the Seas — Grand Caribbean Hotel**, P.O. Box 1850, Route 115, km 12.2, Rincón, PR. (𝄐) 866-274-6266 or 787-823-7500, ✎ 787-823-7501, ▢ www.rinconoftheseas.com, info@rinconoftheseas.com

($) **Very Pricey** (🍽) **BP** (CC) 112 rooms

The owners of this new resort aimed to incorporate an eclectic yet classy swirl of styles. Judging from the lobby, which contains marble columns imported from Oman, and the art deco décor that's peppered with furniture and artwork from India, Pakistan, and Indonesia, their creation was a success. Although many places are more effective at sticking to one theme, Rincón of the Seas is a wonderful resort, highlighted by an expansive pool area and an excellent beach. Despite the Asian and art deco influences, there is still a tropical feel here, thanks to the flowers and hand-painted murals. The rooms are located in three wings that overlook the pool and the sea. There are a few classes of accommodations. We prefer the Deluxe Ocean View rooms (on the upper three floors) — they are equipped with king-size bed, a/c, satellite TV, high-speed

Internet access, minibar, coffeemaker, iron, and hairdryer. The Art Deco Suite includes a sofa bed and DVD player. Each room has a private lanai with sliding glass doors and comfy furniture for enjoying the view. There is a small video arcade and gym, but our favorite feature is the clean expanse of beach with its overhanging palms and great sunsets. The 4,000-square-foot free-form pool has a swim-up bar and café, but the fine dining takes place in the Royal Palm Cafe. Rain is the name of the trendy wine bar — it presents a jungle theme and super-comfortable chairs, although it is open only during the peak season. With an injection of style into a resort mold, Rincón of the Seas offers an exuberant getaway for sun-loving guests.

Rincón Beach Resort, Route 115, km 5.8, Añasco, PR.
ⓒ 866-589-0009 or 787-589-9000 ✎ 787-589-9040,
💻 www.rinconbeach.com, reservations@rinconbeach.com

💲 **Wicked Pricey** ⑪ **EP** ⃝CC 116 rooms

Located on its own desolate beach, this Puerto Rican–owned resort is a pleasant place at which to take a time-out. The rooms are housed in one of three buildings, and many have views overlooking the beach. The resort also offers villas, which include a dining room, kitchen, and living room — best for families or larger groups. The rooms come equipped with phone, cable TV, iron, hairdryers, and a/c, although they also have fans for those of us who crave fresh sea breezes. The layout of the resort is well designed, with a wide-open lobby that offers guests a place to grab a drink and relax. Through the arch is a path leading to the horizon pool and beach area, which is fully equipped with sun chairs. There is no dearth of food or drink at the Rincón Beach Resort — in addition to a swim-up pool bar and boutique wine bar, the casual Pelican Bar & Grill serves lunch, and Las Brasas Restaurant offers a great selection of Latino fusion cuisine for dinner. We recommend the lamb chops with mint sauce or the local favorite, mashed fried plantains stuffed with fresh seafood and topped with creole sauce. Another plus is the oversize chess board with 2-foot-tall pieces — it gives new meaning to the expression "Get in the game!"

Villa Cofresí, P.O. Box 874, Route 115, km 12.0, Rincón, PR.
  © 787-823-2450, ✆ 787-823-1770, 🖥 www.villacofresi.com, info@villacofresi.com

🔳 **Not So Cheap** 🍴 **EP** ⓒⓒ 87 rooms

Villa Cofresí sits right on a great swimming beach. Motelish in look with no visual or ambient appeal, the clean and simple rooms all include a/c, cable TV, a phone, and a fridge. The large rooms have tile floors, dropped ceilings, and all-tile baths with new fixtures. All of the recently added rooms face the ocean. A restaurant, a bar, and a pool that abuts the beach (always a nice touch) round out the facilities. Don't expect a groovy crowd here, but it's reasonably priced and right smack dab on the beach. Anti-chic seekers (or beach bums) might like this place. The hotel's restaurant, Ana de Cofresí, serves seafood, steaks, and traditional Puerto Rican cuisine from 5 to 10 p.m. The villa also offers on-site kayaking, jet skiing, and banana boat rides.

The Lazy Parrot, P.O. Box 430, Route 413, km 4.1, Rincón, PR.
  © 800-294-1752 or 787-823-5654, ✆ 787-823-0224,
  🖥 www.lazyparrot.com, lzparrot@lazyparrot.com

🔳 **Not So Cheap** 🍴 **CP** ⓒⓒ 11 rooms

For those looking to sacrifice beachside location for cheaper prices, the Lazy Parrot is a decent option. Located up in La Cadena hills, this Puerto Rican–owned inn offers great panoramic views and has a refreshing pool area to help you escape the heat. The beach is half a mile down the hill. The rooms are unique, though not overflowing with flavor. Seven of the 11 rooms have a balcony, and we prefer the four upstairs, due to their panoramic view of the sea and green hills behind. The rooms have terra-cotta tile floors, no phone, cable TV, and a/c, but the double beds aren't exactly like floating on a

cloud (don't say we didn't warn you). Room 10 is our favorite
—next time we will bring our own mattress! With its well-
proportioned pool, limited number of rooms, tiki garden,
Smilin' Joe's Restaurant, and Rum Shack Bar, the Lazy Parrot
can be a fun spot to stay. (With names like Smilin' Joe's and
Rum Shack, how can it not be fun?)

Parador Villa Antonio, P.O. Box 68, Route 115, km 12.0, Rincón,
PR. ✆ 800-443-0266 or 787-823-2645, ✎ 787-823-3380,
🖳 www.villa-antonio.com, pva@villa-antonio.com

💲 **Cheap** and up 🍴 **EP** Ⓒ🄲 62 rooms

One of the *paradores* of Puerto Rico, Villa Antonio is next door
to Villa Cofresí. What it lacks in ambiance—its low, squat,
pink buildings aren't very visually appealing—it makes up for
with a wonderful swimming beach. Units are of the one- or
two-bedroom apartment variety and are air-conditioned and
have kitchenettes. The room décor is similar to basic motel
style, with phones, a/c, cable TV, daily maid service, and lanais. There are two pools, a children's play area, a game room,
and two tennis courts, but no restaurant. Wi-Fi is available
throughout much of the property (but not in the rooms), and
there is no on-site restaurant. It's a good budget choice for
families.

Beside the Pointe, P.O. Box 4430, HC-01, Route 413, km 4, Rincón,
PR. ✆ and ✎ 787-823-8550 or 888-823-8550,
🖳 www.besidethepointe.com, info@besidethepointe.com

💲 **Not So Cheap** 🍴 **EP** Ⓒ🄲 8 rooms

Located right on Punta Higuero Beach (or Sandy Beach, as it
is called by non-Spanish speakers), this is a surfer's mecca.
The downstairs is the popular Tamboo Seaside Grill and Tamboo Tavern, so there is never a lack of social life here. In fact,
this is the cultural nexus of the beach, so if you want to jump
into the scene, look no farther. For those who crave tranquillity, some of the aforementioned options might be better
suited. This was once just a surfer's spot but has recently
been spruced up to attract a more moneyed crowd. As a

result, the eight rooms are not too fancy, but they are a step up from the Casa Verde (below). Each has a/c and cable TV, and the three suites feature a small kitchen. We prefer the upstairs rooms, which have their own lanais with sea views. Room 8 is the best — it has not one but two balconies — perfect for those sea-loving couples (who might be in need of a slight break from each other). Free Wi-Fi is available throughout most of the grounds.

Casa Verde, P.O. Box 1102, Route 413, Barrio Puntas, Rincón, PR. ✆ 787-605-5351 or 787-823-3756, 🖳 www.enrincon.com, enrincon@caribe.net

🔳 **Dirt Cheap** 🍴 **EP** CC 8 rooms

This no-frills guesthouse has been one of Rincón's cheapest and most popular places to stay for years. In other words, it's a good party spot. Frequented by lots of surfers who are attracted to the rock-bottom prices and easy beach access, Casa Verde has never needed to do much publicity. The rooms are on the first or second floor of a concrete block–like structure and won't be featured in any fancy magazines. However, they are clean and comfortable. It's run as part of the Rock Bottom Bar & Grill, and there is always a mix of interesting people passing through. Casa Verde has a studio, equipped with a kitchen, as well as one- or two-bedroom suites with a/c, TV, fan, arched doorways, and terra-cotta tile floors. Some rooms open onto a shared veranda with hammocks. The rooms are just steps from the beach and are even closer to the bar that churns out tropical drinks well into the night.

Where to Eat

$$$$$ ✪ **Horned Dorset**, Route 429, km 3, 823-4030

The Horned Dorset offers superb French dining along the Caribbean coast. The food is extremely expensive but impeccably prepared, with a menu that changes daily. We had Peruvian seviche, sauteed foie gras, and lobster tail with pineapple relish — and those were just three of the seven courses!

Meals are well over $100 a person, but they are exquisitely presented in the elegant dining room. Expect only the best. Dress is formal.

$$$ **Las Colinas**, at Parador J. B. Hidden Village, Route 4416, km 2.5, Sector Villa Rubia in neighboring Aguada, 868-8686
For a real Puerto Rican dining experience, check out this place—it's famous for its *churrasco* (grilled meats) and *mofongo* (mashed green plantains). Open Sunday through Thursday from 5 to 11 p.m. and Friday and Saturday from 3 to 11 p.m.

$$ **Lazy Parrot**, Route 413, km 4.1, 823-5654
This hilltop perch (get it?) has great views and pretty good food as well. Its menu is mixed, including good vegetarian options.

$$ **Rock Bottom Bar & Grill**, on Sandy Beach, 605-5351 or 823-3756
Operating as part of the Casa Verde, this is another popular eatery that features happy-hour specials and tasty dinners, specializing in fresh fish. It has a good vibe and churns out a lot of tropical drinks well into the night.

$$ **The Spot @ Black Eagle**, Route 413, km 1, 823-3510
This a good weekend hangout, offering happy-hour specials and sophisticated snacks like grilled snapper with lemon sofrito sauce and hummus with grilled eggplant, goat cheese, and mint served with pita bread. Open during high season only.

$$ ✪ **Tamboo,** on Sandy Beach next to Beside the Pointe, 823-8550
This surf spot offers alfresco lunch and dinner, with views of the sea and its surfers. We were told to steer clear of the burgers, so we opted for a shrimp salad. At night, the activity pulses with DJs and cheap drinks. On Saturday there is live music. This place also happens to be the biggest party spot in

Rincón, although there is also plenty of action at the bar above Casa Verde as well.

⊛Isabela

Isabela, located in the northwest corner of the island, is a new feature in our Puerto Rico book. Thanks to its beautiful beaches, this region (including the nearby settlements of Aguada and Aguadilla) is undergoing a tourism boom. In short, it's an ideal beach retreat — the shore here is much less developed than in other parts of Puerto Rico. For centuries, Isabela was a tobacco-growing town, but today people come for its smokin' coastline (we couldn't resist). Desolate beaches give way to rolling sand dunes and limestone cliffs. The natural beauty here provides the perfect backdrop for nature-oriented activities such as kayaking or horseback riding. For equestrians, **Tropical Trails** (872-9256) offers amazing two-hour $35 guided rides through the almond forest and along the beach. Shacks Beach is perhaps the best spot on Puerto Rico for windsurfing or kitesurfing, and the waves at Jobos Beach are ideal for surfers. **Hang Loose Surf Shop** (872-2490) can help arrange gear for any of these activities.

What makes this place so special (and an undiscovered gem) is the fact that there is so much coastline that has yet to be developed. With a rental car, it's easy to cruise along and stake out your own little slice of paradise at which to spend the day. We love Montones, Bajuras, and Sardinera Beach as well. In Jobos, ask for **El Pozo de Jacinto** — it is a blowhole in the rocks that looms over a swirl of oceanic turbulence. The nearby **Guajataca Forest** is noteworthy for its geological formations of limestone. *Karst* is the word used to describe this inland terrain, which is quite rugged and surreal-looking at times. Route 446 rings through the forest and is a beautiful drive; there is a lookout tower as well. Close by is Lake Guajataca, formed by a dam, which is a popular fishing site. Although there is still not much in terms of restaurants or nightlife, the allure of Isabela is starting to turn heads, and it definitely caught our attention — this is one of our favorite places on the island. The best dive shop in town is **Aquatica** (890-6071).

Where to Stay

Villa Montaña Beach Resort, Road 4466, km 1.9, Barrio Bajuras, Isabela, PR. © 888-780-9195 or 787-872-9554, ✆ 787-872-9553, ☐ www.villamontana.com, frontdesk@villamontana.com

💲 **Ridiculous** 🍴 **EP** ⒸⒸ 78 rooms

The mantra at Villa Montaña seems to be that good taste need not equal extravagance. We like that mantra, and as a result we are very high on this beach resort. Unlike at many resorts that boast hundreds of rooms and an unlimited number of amenities, the French and Spanish owners here have focused instead on creating a more intimate sense of luxury. Set on 26 acres along a pristine beach, the resort is spread out among its manicured grounds. Instead of being a blocklike hotel right on the beach, it has preserved harmony with nature. The beach naturally gives way to a beautiful lawn peppered with palms and tropical plants.

Guests can choose hotel rooms or villas that range from one to three bedrooms. The villas are exquisite: Brushed pastel stucco walls adjoin cathedral-style ceilings. We love the Jacuzzis in the bathrooms (be sure to request one when making reservations) and the open-air showers. The villas also come with climate-control a/c, ceiling fans, and digital cable TV. They vary in size, but all have kitchens and queen-size sofa beds in the living room. The one-bedroom villa is ideal for four people. We prefer the Ocean Villas, which are right on the beach. The hotel's rooms (as opposed to its villas) are built into a cliff that's situated a bit off the beach, but they are blessed with sea views and an endless ocean breeze. Each is equipped with a queen-size bed and a terrace with chairs.

The stylish pool is embellished with Asian elevated sofas and wide sun chairs, all topped with plush purple cushions. The Eclipse Restaurant is an open-air experience that is classy yet casual. Due to its new Puerto Rican chef's experience in France and California, the Eclipse now specializes in French-Asian-Latino fusion. After a dinner here on the torch-lit terrace overlooking the sea, readers will understand our romantic prologue. The beach out front is an untouched gem of barren beauty, but for those who seek more activities, there is an open-air spa, horseback riding, bikes, kayaks, a rock-climbing wall, and two tennis courts. With tropical plants, birds, and an easygoing atmosphere, the Villa Montaña is an ideal resort at which to enjoy the beauty of Puerto Rico in a naturally harmonious setting.

Parador Villas del Mar Hau, P.O. Box 510, Road 466, km 8.9, Isabela, PR. ℂ 787-872-2045, 787-872-2627, or 787-872-2021, ✺ 787-830-4988, 🖥 www.paradorvillasdelmarhau.com, villahau@prtc.net

💲 **Not So Cheap** ⑪ **EP** ⒸⒸ 43 units

With a setting as splendid as this, it didn't take much to wow us. Located right on the picturesque bay of Playa Montones — one of the most beautiful little beaches in all of Puerto Rico — this unassuming collection of wooden *cabañas* provides just enough comfort for a very relaxing and unpretentious vacation spot. We cannot boast enough about this beach. Palms and pines compete for space on the shores of this horseshoe bay, whose serene waters are perfect for swimming. For those looking to enjoy a gorgeous beach without the pomp and circumstance of a big resort, the brightly colored cottages here are ideal and very affordable. The cottages come equipped with cable TV and a/c, but they also have fans and screen doors that allow for a sea breeze. Each has a full kitchen, a sitting room with a sofa bed, and a bedroom. The porches are huge, complete with table, chairs, and barbeque grill. There are also studios, which are more traditional hotel rooms housed in two-story wooden huts — they have their own terrace, cable TV, a/c, and fan. With fewer than 50 units, there is never a big crowd here.

The hotel grounds include tennis courts, a sand volleyball court, and a small pool out back, and with a beach like this, we were in heaven. The seaside Olas y Arena Restaurant is a great spot at which to enjoy the sea breeze over a tropical dinner. The Villas del Mar Hau has traded silly amenities for pure, natural beauty, which suits true beach lovers like us just fine.

Costa Dorada Beach Resort, 900 Calle Emilio González, Road 466, km 0.1, Isabela, PR. ✆ 877-975-0101 or 787-872-7255, ✆ 787-872-7595, 🖥 www.costadoradabeach.com, info@costadoradabeach.com

💲 **Pricey** 🍴 **EP** CC 52 rooms

Judging from the brochure or Web site, this place looks like a Caribbean jewel. However, the Costa Dorada is in fact a very tacky, run-of-the-mill resort. Our main gripe here is the layout —the rooms are crammed together tightly in tall concrete blocks, which takes away from the relaxing seaside experience we crave. Many don't have sea views but instead face the measly pool area. Although it's billed as a "beach resort," guests have to walk through a gate and across a street to get to the beach, which seems to have been treated as an afterthought. We have no problem walking a few paces to the beach, but a few chairs out front would be nice. It appears that the pool (which was drained when we stayed here) is the resort's centerpiece, which isn't saying a lot—it is very small and completely lacking in style. It's just a pool and a few chairs—not what we would expect for a resort in this price range.

The rooms have the normal amenities, but the whole place is completely devoid of style or sophistication. We recommend that you save some money and enjoy the natural beauty of the Villas de Mar Hau or drop a few more dollars and upgrade to the Villa Montaña. The resort also offers one- to three-bedroom villas next door, but we were equally unenthused.

Where to Eat

$$$ ⊛ **Eclipse Restaurant**, Villa Montaña Beach Resort, Road 4466, km 1.9, 872-9554

Sure, it is set within a resort, but we love this romantic spot where the waves caress the shore. The restaurant fits gracefully into the natural setting, and the food is excellent, too.

Dinners are candlelit, and the cuisine is a fusion of European and Caribbean.

$$ **Happy Belly's,** Jobos Beach, 872-6566
This beachside sports bar and grill is good fun. The food is basic but tasty. It has great views and happy-hour specials, too.

$$$ **Mesón Gastronómico El Pescador,** Carretera 466, Bo Villa Pesquera, 872-1343
Don't call it a restaurant—it's a Mesón Gastronómico, which is the Puerto Rican connotation for exceptional cuisine. If a kitchen cooks up creole food this delicious, we don't care what it's called. It's set right on the beach. The seafood is the best option here, and the weekday lunch buffet is quite a spread as well.

DON'T MISS

⊛ El Yunque

You can't visit Puerto Rico without a visit to El Yunque (officially the Caribbean National Forest and part of the U.S. National Forest system). It is a great example of a rainforest for those who have never seen one before, although it was ravaged by 1998's Hurricane Georges. Evidence of the deadly storm is apparent everywhere, but in the tropics recovery is remarkably quick.

El Yunque is only about an hour's drive east of San Juan, and it is almost impossible to drive to the summit (which was possible before Hurricanes Hugo and Georges). The drive up to the visitors' center takes you past towering banks of green ferns and canopies of trees and vines. The forest itself consists of 28,000 acres and is the largest and wettest in the U.S. National Forest system (240 inches, or 100 billion gallons, of water fall on the forest every year). Note that there are no poisonous snakes in Puerto Rico. Be sure to stop at the **Sierra Palma**, an interpretive center located at km 11.6 on Route 91, just before the parking area, for information on the hiking trails; open daily from 9:30 a.m. to 5 p.m., except on Christmas Day (787-888-1880).

If you decide to hike (you should), the first section of the trail to the summit of El Yunque is a well-worn concrete path. Though a steady climb, it is fairly easy but very humid (remember—*rain*forest). The second section turns into a path, which, though a little muddy, is rather easy to walk. If you walk at a steady pace, you can make it to the summit in one hour (we did). For the length of the trail, you will be walking through forest. Some people might be over the whole concept in 15 minutes and will turn around. The few vista points you come to, including the towers, are more often than not shrouded in clouds, so don't expect spectacular vistas; expect the forest and its hundreds of varieties of foliage and birds (which you hear more often than see). In this age of sound bites and short attention spans, if you don't like the forest you will be bored fairly quickly. Once you get near the top, there is a choice—you'll reach a fork in the road. We recommend going to the tower, which is just a few hundred yards away. The temptation is to go to the peak of El Yunque, because it is the summit. However, when you get to the peak, there are at least seven huge microwave transmission towers to thoroughly radiate you (or at least there were before Hurricane Georges). Since the clouds usually block the view, these lovely structures will be what you see. The only advantage to going to the peak is that you can take the road down (open to official vehicles only), which is a faster route.

Bioluminescent Bays

On moonless nights, some of Puerto Rico's bays come alive with incredible "underwater fireworks" caused by millions of bioluminescent organisms that light up the sea. It is an amazing sight to behold. In addition to Vieques's well-known bioluminescent bay, there are two on the main island that also merit checking out. One is in Fajardo and the other is at La Parguera, the fishing village near Guánica. There are plenty of local tour agencies that offer cheap excursions to witness this natural spectacle.

Scenic Drives

There are several nice drives on this very scenic island. The two we would recommend are a half-day and an overnight journey from San Juan, respectively.

   Trip 1 takes you east on **Route 3 to Luquillo**, the location of a great local beach (the drive between San Juan and Luquillo is pretty hideous), and south past Fajardo and the very pretty Playa de Nagua-bo. It continues on Route 3 past industrial Humacao and into sugar-cane territory. When you get to Yabucoa, you start to climb through some very winding mountain roads with great vistas of the valley and the sea (watch out for the cane trucks — don't worry, you'll hear their horns). The road descends to Maunabo and eventually follows the sea along the Caribbean. When you get to Guayama, take Route 15 north to Cayey. This is incredibly scenic — lots of mountain vistas and lush foliage and vegetation. At Cayey, get on Route 52 and head north back to San Juan.

Trip 2 takes you through the **Cordillera Central**, the mountainous spine of Puerto Rico. This is a long, twist-and-turn drive, so leave early in the morning for a relaxing pace. Arrange to stay in Boquerón or Rincón at the other end of the road. Take Route 52 south from San Juan, get off in Cayey, and take Route 14 to Coamo and the **Baños de Coamo** (hot springs), where you can enjoy a natural hot tub. From Coamo, take Route 150 west past Lago Tao Vaga, through the tiny town of Villaba. At Villaba, head north on Route 149 until you reach the junction of Route 143. Turn left (west) to enjoy this stretch of ma-jestic scenery. This road will take you past the biggest mountains in Puerto Rico, including Cerro de Punta, Puerto Rico's highest peak at 4,390 feet. At the junction of Route 10 (not the highway under con-struction, but the secondary road just beyond), head north until you get to Route 518. If you've had enough and there is enough daylight left for you to head back to San Juan (you'll need at least three hours), continue on Route 10 (it will eventually meet the completed part of Highway 10, which you should take) until you reach the junction of Route 22, then go east on 22. If you want to continue, take Route 518 to Route 525. About 3 miles later is the junction of Route 135. Turn left (west) on Route 135 until the junction of Route 128. Turn left (south) again on Route 128 and follow to Route 365. Take Route 365, which will merge with Route 366. At the junction of Route 120, turn right (north) onto Route 120 and continue until you come to Route 106. Turn left (west) onto Route 106 and follow this all the way to Mayagüez. Once you are in Mayagüez, Route 2 North takes you to the Rincón area, and Route 2 South takes you to Route 100 to Boquerón.

Río Camuy Cave Park

Everyone raves about these "oh, you've got to see them" caves. Personally, the last thing we want to do in the tropics is go subterranean. However, they are a wonder, and kids will love them. They are located near Lares, and tours are usually conducted via trolley. We prefer the more adventurous option, which includes rappelling or hiking to the center of the Cueva Catedral, which was recently opened to the public. This cave contains 14th-century petroglyphs as well. Tours run two hours. Open Wednesday from 8 a.m. to 3 p.m. You must call ahead to reserve a space on the tour (787-898-3100 or 787-763-0568). The cost is $10 for adults, $7 for children.

Arecibo Observatory

Home of the world's largest radio telescope (the radar dish is over 1,000 feet in diameter, 565 feet deep, and covers 20 acres), the observatory and its scientists listen for signs of life in the universe. It is part of the National Astronomy and Ionosphere Center and is operated by Cornell University in conjunction with the National Science Foundation. Viewers of several movies, including *Contact* and an early 007 movie whose name we can't remember, will recognize the dish. A new visitors' center has a cool "More Than Meets the Eye" interactive exhibit and a great view of the observatory. Open Wednesday through Friday from noon to 4 p.m., weekends and holidays from 9 a.m. to 4 p.m. Admission is $5 for adults and $3 for kids and seniors. Call 787-878-2612 for more information.

Casa Bacardi Visitor Center

Any place that churns out 100,000 gallons of liquor per day can spare a few samples here and there, and that is just the way it is at this famous rum distillery. Opened in 2000, the visitors' center offers an informative 45-minute tour of the distillery, and, of course, the gift shop—funny how that always seems to happen. Come see why Bacardi has made Puerto Rico the rum capital of the world (or so it claims). It's located at Bay View Industrial Park, Road 888, km 2.6, Cataño; phone 788-8400. Tours are offered Monday through Saturday from 8:30 a.m. to 5:30 p.m. (last tour at 4:15 p.m.) and Sunday from 10 a.m. to 3 p.m. (last tour at 3:45 p.m.), free of charge.

Nature Resort

In a jungle-like mountain setting in Utuado (near the Camuy Caves) is **Hotel La Casa Grande** (888-343-2272, 787-894-3939, or 787-894-3900, www.hotelcasagrande.com). Once the hacienda for a 5,000-acre ranch, the old house and its surroundings have been turned into a 20-room inn and restaurant by ex–New Yorkers Steven and Marlene Weingarten. Folks are all abuzz about this place, which was the winner of the Green Inn Award in 1999, 2004, and 2006.

✪ Windsurfing and Surfing in Rincón

If you're a windsurfer or surfer, this is one of the best places to do both in the Caribbean. Many championships in both sports are held at Surfer and Wilderness Beaches, and there is a growing California-style surfer community.

Guánica

This is a wonderful and scenic town for those in search of the real Puerto Rico (see Guánica section).

Lunch at Hostería del Mar and Dinner at Pamela's

Our favorite spots for lunch and dinner in San Juan are in Ocean Park (see Where to Eat).

Culebra and Vieques

These two small islands off the east coast of Puerto Rico offer a fun day trip, overnight excursion, or entire holiday. See the Culebra and Vieques chapters.

Qué Pasa?

Published by the Puerto Rico Tourism Company, this is a great free publication to peruse for events and the latest info. It has an ample listing of hotels and restaurants in Puerto Rico. For a free copy, call 800-223-6530 from the United States or 721-2400 in Puerto Rico. You can visit either the *Qué Pasa* Web site at www.qpsm.com or the Puerto Rico Tourism Company Web site at www.gotopuertorico .com.

Ponce Museum of Art

Designed by famous architect Edward Durrel Stone, this building is worth a visit for the design alone, which is reminiscent of the Greek

Parthenon. With more than 850 paintings, 800 sculptures, and 500 prints highlighting 500 years of Western art, this museum is a must-see for art enthusiasts. Look for featured exhibitions of Latin American artists. Open daily from 10 a.m. to 5 p.m.; phone 848-0505.

Museo de Arte de Puerto Rico

Opened in 2000, the museum incorporates part of the old San Juan Municipal Hospital designed in the neoclassical style by William Shimmelphening with a brand new modern architectural five-story gem designed by Otto Reyes and Luis Guiterrez. The museum has more than 130,000 square feet of exhibition space and a three-story atrium called the Great Hall. Puerto Rican art throughout the island's history is on display here. Finally, Puerto Rico has a world-class art exhibition space! Located at 299 Avenida de Diego in Santurce, it's open Tuesday through Saturday from 10 a.m. to 5 p.m., Wednesday until 8 p.m., and Sunday from 11 a.m. to 6 p.m. Admission is $5 for adults and $3 for kids and seniors. Call 787-977-6277 or go to www.mapr.org for more info.

Surfing

Puerto Rico is home to excellent surf breaks all year round. In the winter, the waves at Rincón are sensational. This is the premier surf location on the island—surfers are drawn to breaks such as The Landing, Punta Higuero, and Sandy Beach. Around the lighthouse are even more gnarly waves, sometimes up to 20 feet high. For those interested in seeking out these giant waves, just ask for Tres Palmas. But Rincón is not the only surf spot. Even San Juan itself has great surf from November through February—this is evident from all the high school kids playing hooky. In the city, our favorite surf spots are Isla Verde Beach (just east of the Ritz-Carlton Hotel) and Aviones, which is in Piñones. On the east coast, check out La Pared in Luquillo or El Convento in Fajardo. Those staying at the Four Points Sheraton in Palmas del Mar (Humacao) will find great breaks as well. Some of the best spots, though, are along less traveled beaches. The stretch between Hatillo and Arecibo along the northern coast has some great breaks, in particular Hollows and La Marina. Isabela's surf scene is being discovered as we speak—there are already surf schools popping up, and for good reason. Jobos Beach here is perhaps the best break on the island, which is why international competitions are held here. Farther west toward Aguadilla are several other great surf spots, such as Gas Chambers and the aptly named Surfer's Beach.

Culebra

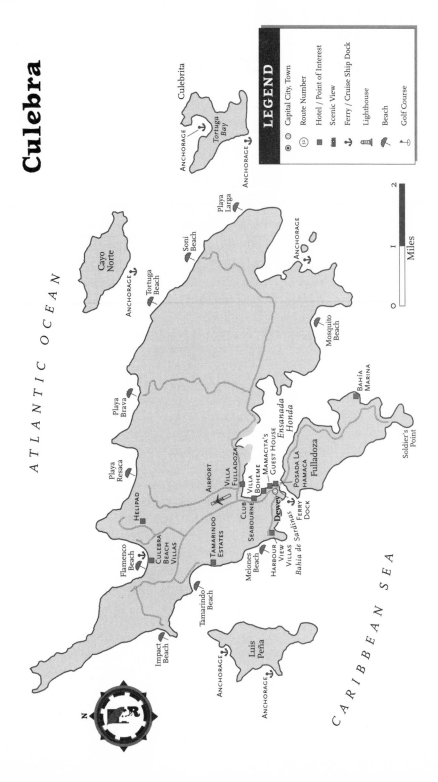

Culebra

TOURISTO SCALE:

👙👙👙 (3)

Many years back, on one of our first trips to Culebra, we were picked up at the airport by a "limo" in the form of a beat-up old VW van with no doors and two plastic deck chairs for seats. On our most recent visit, we were greeted by a beat-up old van *with* doors. How nice it was to see that not much has changed here! Welcome to Culebra — the land of the *very* laid-back. Perhaps more than any other island in the Caribbean, Culebra is dominated by its natural wonders. Tourism here is not focused on fancy restaurants or five-star hotels. Instead, the major attraction here is the beaches, which are scattered around this island gem. Culebra is actually a collection of tiny islands and cays, and most of it is a national wildlife refuge, home to large colonies of migratory birds and marine life such as endangered sea turtles. Don't expect much, however — Culebra is a small and simple place. Although politically it is part of the Commonwealth of Puerto Rico, it is light-years away from the fast pace of San Juan. Spanish is the primary language here, but English is spoken everywhere. The main village on the island is Dewey, named for Admiral George Dewey, an American officer in the Spanish-American War. This is where the ferry, the post office, and most of

Culebra: Key Facts

Location	18°N by 65°W
	17 miles east of Fajardo, Puerto Rico
	12 miles west of St. Thomas
	1,660 miles southeast of New York
Size	7 miles long by 3 miles wide
Highest point	Mt. Resaca (650 feet)
Population	About 2,000
Language	Spanish, English
Time	Atlantic Standard Time (1 hour ahead of EST, same as EDT)
Area code	787 (must be dialed with all calls locally)
Electricity	110 volts AC, 60 cycles
Currency	The U.S. dollar
Driving	On the right; valid driver's license okay
Documents	None for Americans and no Customs hassles, either. Canadians need a passport if traveling by air, or proof of nationality (birth certificate, certificate of citizenship and government-issued photo ID) if arriving by sea. By January 2008, Canadians will need a passport even if traveling by sea. Brits need a visa unless they hold an e-passport or a passport conforming to certain other specific U.S. government requirements. (Check with the U.S. Consulate or your travel agent for more specifics.)
Departure tax	None
Beer to drink	Medalla
Rum to drink	Don Q or Bacardi
Music to hear	Rock, reggae, salsa, and *reggaetón*
Tourism info	800-223-6530 or 787-742-1033
	www.culebra-island.com
	www.culebra.org
	www.enchanted-isle.com

the commerce is located. There are only a few hundred hotel rooms on the island—which has only about 3,000 inhabitants—a few good restaurants, and no real nightclubs, discos, or casinos. The pace is slow, slow, slow! Overall, one gets the impression that this is what the Caribbean as a whole used to be like. Indeed, Culebrenses—as residents are called—are very covetous of their way of life and are very suspect of any change or "progress." Their attitude is "leave us alone." So far, they've been successful. Actually, Hurricanes Hugo (1989), Luís (1995), and Georges (1998) have helped their cause tremendously by hurting the flourishing tourist trade with both damaged accommodations and bad publicity.

Culebra is not a lush, verdant island. Rather, it's very arid. However, its star attraction, besides its isolation, is its beaches. Despite its beautiful beaches, Culebra is not for everyone. It's rustic, and if you expect to be pampered or entertained, forget it, it's not for you. But if you don't mind simple accommodations, cooking for yourself a lot or eating at mostly simple restaurants, and tons of quiet, then you'll love it. Probably the best analogy is that of a Cinderella who doesn't want to go to the ball. She purposely stays out of the spotlight cast on her star stepsisters, Puerto Rico and St. Thomas, loving the solitude. She is one of the Caribbean's best-kept secrets—an island where the pace is that of yesteryear, the beaches are gorgeous, and attitude nonexistent.

The Briefest History

Culebra was not inhabited by Europeans until the very late date of 1886, when it was settled by the Spanish (it was part of the Spanish Virgin Islands). It was ceded to the United States as part of the settlement of the Spanish-American War. The United States incorporated it into the Commonwealth of Puerto Rico, where it has remained ever since. In 1909 President Theodore Roosevelt designated the former Spanish Crown lands (2,800 acres) a national wildlife refuge, to protect the native seabird colonies. Nevertheless, the U.S. Navy used it for bombing practice from World War II until 1975. Today this area is administered by the U.S. Fish and Wildlife Service.

Getting There

San Juan is the primary gateway to the Caribbean and is reached by most major U.S. carriers. From San Juan and Fajardo, Vieques Air Link (www.vieques-island.com/val, 888-901-9247 stateside, 787-741-8331 in Isla Verde and San Juan, 787-742-0254 in Culebra, and 787-863-3020 in Fajardo) has regularly scheduled service from Luis Muñoz Marín Airport and the smaller, domestic Isla Grande Airport (convenient for anyone staying in Old San Juan or the Condado). Air Flamenco (www.airflamenco.net, 787-724-1818) offers daily flights from Isla Grande Airport as well. Isla Nena (www.islanena.8m.com; 877-812-5144 stateside, 787-863-3075 in San Juan) also has charter service, some scheduled service from San Juan's Luis Muñoz Marín International Airport, and hourly trips to Fajardo. It also occasionally flies from Vieques to Culebra if there is demand. If you're interested in chartering a flight, Air America (www.airamericacaribbean.com, 787-276-5669) offers one-way, five-person flights for $450 or nine-person flights for $900. For those who don't want to fly, there is passenger and car ferry service from Fajardo daily, with at least three ferries a day going back and forth; call the Fajardo Port Authority at 787-742-3161 or 787-863-0705 for the current schedules. Also, there is a seasonal Fast Ferry service available from Old San Juan to Culebra that takes under two hours. The one-way cost is $42; the round-trip fare is $69. Contact Island Hi-Speed Ferry at 877-899-3993 or www.islandhispeedferry.com more information.

Getting Around

Although there is good minivan taxi service (*públicos*) between Dewey and Playa Flamenco, a jeep or car is a good idea for getting to other beaches, the grocery store, and just general mobility. There are several outfits who rent cars, including Prestige Car Rental (787-742-3242), Jerry's Jeeps (787-742-0587), R & W Jeep Rental (787-742-0563), Carlos Jeep Rental (787-742-3514), Coral Reef Car Rental (787-742-0055), Dick & Cathy (787-742-0062), and Tamarindo Car Rental (787-742-3343). For scooters, try JM Rental (742-0521). There is a full-service bike shop in Dewey called Culebra Bike Shop (787-742-2209), which rents mountain bikes. Dick & Cathy (787-742-0062) also rents bikes.

Focus on Culebra: The Beaches

For such a small island, there are some amazing beaches here. The lack of development has saved most of them from the usual Caribbean resort blight. Two of the beaches, **Resaca** and **Brava**, are nesting sites for leatherback turtles and are off-limits from April 1 to August 30. They are also hard to get to (the best way is by boat), but they are great for hikers. Since shade is minimal at all Culebra beaches, be sure to bring a beach umbrella so you don't get burned to a crisp.

We vacillate between which is the best beach on the island, Zoni or Flamenco. Several years ago, in an early edition of *Rum & Reggae's Caribbean*, we decided it was **Zoni** (also spelled Soni), at the eastern end of the island, with its wide stretch of white sand, calm surf, and no people. There are great views of the islets of Culebrita and Cayo Norte across the bay, and far in the distance you can see St. Thomas. To get to Zoni, take the eastern road as far as it will go. You will see cars parked where the road gets really bad. Park there and walk the remaining 100 yards down to the beach. There are no facilities and no shade at the beach, so be sure to bring water and an umbrella.

In a more recent edition of *Rum & Reggae's Caribbean*, we changed our minds (we have that right, don't we?). We're now mad for Flamenco, Culebra's most popular strand and again our favorite. In fact, we rate ⊛**Playa Flamenco** as the best beach not only in Puerto Rico but in all the Caribbean (if it is even fair to do such a thing). A mile-long arc of totally white, powdery sand set in a large cove, this is truly a beautiful beach. Its exposure to the northern Atlantic allows for good bodysurfing, especially in the winter months. It can get busy on summer weekends and during Puerto Rican holidays. At the parking area there are restrooms and picnic tables. If you walk to the left, you'll come to a very secluded part of the beach, especially if you go around the rocky coral point. On the western end of the beach is Culebra Beach Villas & Resort, a camp lodge–like place with a beach bar that's popular with Puerto Rican families. Playa Flamenco is also the only area in Culebra that allows ⊛camping. Though not exactly a site of wilderness camping, the campground is located in a pretty area right near the water and is government run to ensure safety. To get to Flamenco, take the road that passes the airport (the runway will be on your right) and follow it to the end.

Other beaches to explore on the island are **Soldado** (great for scuba or snorkeling), **Tamarindo** (known for its brain coral and parrotfish), **Impact** (great snorkeling), and **Tortuga** (very private). **Carlos Rosario Beach** also has some of the best snorkeling, whereas Brava Beach has the best waves. There is also a wonderful little beach on the islet of Luis Peña. Culebrita, a cay located just off of Culebra, has two gorgeous beaches and many tidal pools that offer the best ⊛snorkeling around. Culebrita can only be reached by boat. We recommend hiring **Muff the Magic Fun Boat**—talk to Jack or Pat (787-397-7497).

Where to Stay

Accommodations are much more basic in Culebra than on most Caribbean islands, but many options offer a stylish appeal. We like Club Seabourne and some of the guesthouses in Dewey, such as Villa Boheme, Posada La Hamaca, and Mamacita's. Despite our general aversion to large-scale resorts in Culebra, we were fans of the 164-room Costa Bonita Beach Resort, but it recently ceased operation, so Culebra's sole attempt at a real "resort" seems to have failed. There are also several condos or villa properties, which may be the best way to go because they come with a kitchen.

Club Seabourne, P.O. Box 357, Calle Fulladoza, Culebra, PR.
℃ 787-742-3169, ✆ 787-742-0210,
🖳 www.clubseabourne.com

💲 **Not So Cheap** 🍴 CP Ⓒⓒ 12 rooms

> We simply adore this inn because of its intimacy and subtle style. A few minutes out of town on Ensenada Bay is this small hotel, which welcomes guests who need to "press the restart button in life." We must admit that this is the ideal place for invigoration. We love the privacy here; the rooms are housed in Old World plantation-style villas set amid tropical

gardens designed by a prominent landscape artist. The fertile grounds include ginger and flamboyan trees and are blooming with color. The villas are done up in refined style with four-poster queen-size beds. They also have a/c and terraces with wondrous vistas. For those traveling with children (or two couples), the Family Villas with two bedrooms are ideal. The recently remodeled main building, designed in tasteful Caribbean style, includes a library and living room with huge TV for movie viewing. The pool has a wonderful view, and the gazebo bar and café offers tasty eats. However, the real attraction, when it comes to food, is the White Sands Restaurant. Its creative Caribbean cuisine makes this one of our favorite spots on the island. Once we tasted the delicious food, we realized that if there is one spot in the Puerto Rico area in which to partake in an all-inclusive package — which is available — this is it. With its exotic and intimate setting, Club Seabourne ranks as one of our favorites.

Villa Boheme, 368 Calle Fulladoza, Culebra, PR. 🕿 and 🖂 787-742-3508, 🖳 www.villaboheme.com, villaboheme@yahoo.com

💲 **Cheap** and up ⑪ **EP** Ⓒⓒ 11 rooms

Set in a nice, breezy location right on Ensenada Bay, this guesthouse is a great place to get an authentic feel for Culebra. It's also within easy walking distance of town and restaurants. A symphony of beige and mauve, all rooms are simple and comfortable and feature a/c, ceiling fans, and private baths. A communal kitchen is available for guests. There are also efficiency apartments with fully equipped kitchens and private lanais. The Villa has a large lanai with chaises and chairs, a great place for a cocktail. This is great choice for windsurfers, who can sail right off the dock in front. This would make a good 007 getaway!

Posada La Hamaca, P.O. Box 388, 68 Calle Castelar, Dewey, Culebra, PR. 🕿 787-435-0028, 🖂 787-742-3516, 🖳 www.posada.com, info@posada.com

💲 **Cheap** ⑪ **EP** Ⓒⓒ 10 rooms

Located right in Dewey on the canal by the drawbridge, Posada La Hamaca was one of the original guesthouses on the island. This wonderfully clean and comfortable place is still a good choice for in-town accommodation, especially since the efficiencies have recently been remodeled. Situated in a simple Spanish-style house are seven double rooms and three efficiency units (i.e., with kitchenettes or kitchens). Each room has a private bath, a/c, and ceiling fan. The Posada provides free ice, coolers, and towels for the beach. The new owners are very friendly and helpful as well.

Mamacita's Guest House, P.O. Box 818, 66 Calle Castelar, Dewey, Culebra, PR. ✆ 787-742-0090, ✉ 787-742-0301, 🖳 www.mamacitaspr.com, info@mamacitaspr.com

💲 **Cheap** ⑪ **EP** 🆑 6 rooms

This is a small, brightly colored guesthouse located right next door to Posada La Hamaca. Mamacita's also has a pretty, colorful patio on the canal, where breakfast, lunch, and dinner are served. There are only six rooms, located above the restaurant in decked spaces. The room on the top floor has the best views, including a sweeping vista of the harbor. All rooms have a/c, private baths, lanais, and ceiling fans and have recently been outfitted with satellite TV. The Caribbean Bar is a great place for a cocktail at sunset (or sunrise, if the urge arises).

Bahía Marina, P.O. Box 807, Playa Sardinas, Punta Soldado Road, km 2.4, Culebra, PR. ✆ 866-CULEBRA or 787-742-0535, ✉ 787-742-0536, 🖳 www.bahiamarina.net, askme@bahiamarina.net

💲 **Pricey** and up ⑪ **EP** 🆑 16 apartments

This relative newcomer to the Culebra scene is not on the beach, yet it's strategically positioned on a bluff overlooking Fulladoza Bay. Where there's a bluff, there is usually a view, and Bahía Marina does not disappoint. In addition to the property's sundeck with panoramic view, each of the one-bedroom, two-bath apartments comes with a private lanai and a full ocean view. Although they are very simple in décor, the apartments are clean and spacious enough to accommodate four people. Each has a fully loaded kitchen, free Wi-Fi, satellite TV, DVD player, and a/c.

The grounds feature two pools, a Jacuzzi, fine dining at the Dakity Restaurant, the lively (by Culebra standards) Shipwreck Bar & Grill, and the always enjoyable Cayo Swim-Up Bistro (only open on weekends). There is casual live music on Saturday. There are no phones in the rooms, but management claims that the property has great cell phone reception. Culebra is not really a cell phone kind of place, so we never turned ours on to see if they were correct. However, we think Bahía Marina is worth the gamble (and if you have the desire to turn on your cell phones, let us know how many bars you get).

Tamarindo Estates, P.O. Box 313, Tamarindo Road, Culebra, PR. Ⓒ 787-742-3343, ✆ 787-742-3342, 🖳 www.tamarindoestates.com
💲 **Pricey** and up 🍴 **EP** ⒸⒸ 12 cottages

These comfortable and affordable one- and two-bedroom cottages are a good option for those in search of simple living near the shores of a secluded beach. Although the units are not actually located on Tamarindo Beach, they are scattered throughout 60 acres of undeveloped land and are just a few minutes on foot to the beach. Tamarindo Estates is the only resort located within Culebra's Marine Reserve and, as such, it takes pride in its avoidance of luxury. Indeed, the rooms are very basic. Basic is fine, but we did find them to be a bit tight on space. There is no housekeeping service, no in-room phone, and the only "frills" are a TV, a/c, and a ceiling fan. Internet is available through one computer for all guests to share (that's fine by us). However, the units are clean and have a private bath, a useful kitchen area, and a covered veranda that offers good views. There is no restaurant on the property, but there is a pool with a decent sundeck and a private beach house with restrooms and showers. In case of problems, there is a full-time, on-site manager. Other than that, you're on your own, so even by Culebra's standards, Tamarindo Estates epitomizes getting away from it all.

Note that the road to Tamarindo Estates has finally been paved, so those who once complained about how difficult it was to get here need whine no more.

Villa Fulladoza, P.O. Box 162, Culebra, PR. ✆ and ✆ 787-742-3576, 🖳 www.culebra-island.com/CulebraIsland/Places_to_Stay/ Villa_Fulladosa/villa_fulladosa.htm

💲 **Cheap** 🍴 **EP** 🆑 7 rooms

Situated right on the water with nice views of Ensenada Honda, this is a popular, interesting, and somewhat eclectically decorated (*homemade* is the word they use to describe the décor) complex within a 10-minute walk of town. Each of the seven units has a fully equipped kitchenette, ceiling and/or floor fans, and private bath. Most of the apartments are for two people, but four of them can accommodate two adults and two children. There is a boat dock and moorings available to those who have boats. It's located bayside, so there is no beach, but there are great views and a personal dock.

Harbour View Villas, P.O. Box 216, Culebra, PR. ✆ 800-440-0070 or 787-742-3855, ✆ 787-742-3171, 🖳 www.culebrahotel.com, info@culebrahotel.com

💲 **Not So Cheap** and up 🍴 **EP** 3 villas and 3 suites

These rather space age–looking villas on stilts sit just outside Dewey on the road to Melones Beach. Large lanais, lots of wood, 12-foot-high ceilings, big windows, and French doors with views of Bahia de Sardinas are the main features. The three villas, a one-bedroom and two two-bedroom, come with fully equipped kitchens, ceiling fans, and a living room. There are also three suites with kitchens, tile baths, and air-conditioned bedrooms at the top of the 5-acre property. You'll want to have a four-wheel-drive vehicle or a lot of nerve to negotiate the steep and treacherous driveway. We find these rustic accommodations to be a lot like a Vermont cabin — with mosquito netting over the beds for pioneer-like protection against the bugs. Nevertheless, the harbor views are spectacular! The restaurant here, Juanita Bananas, is also top-notch. It's run by the owner's daughter and open for dinner. The dishes are well prepared with fresh fruits and vegetables from the garden. No credit cards.

Culebra Beach Villas, Playa Flamenco, Culebra, PR. ℂ 877-767-7575, 787-767-7575, or 787-742-0517, ✆ 787-281-6975, 🖳 www.culebrabeachrental.com, cbrental@prtc.com

💲 **Not So Cheap** and up 🕼 **EP** (CC) 33 units

The best thing about Culebra Beach Villas is the location— right on Playa Flamenco. It looks somewhat like a ski lodge with satellite cabins and is popular with Puerto Rican families. Don't expect much, as *rustic* is the buzzword here. However, the management is friendly, and there's that gorgeous beach in front. The units (18 in concrete villas, 15 in a multistory hotel) come with basic amenities like a fridge, microwave, stove, a/c, barbecue, TV, and private bath. The property's Coconuts Beach Grill sits right on the beach and is a fine place for snacks or tropical libations.

Where to Eat

There aren't many choices, and don't expect haute cuisine. Here's what we recommend.

$$ **Coconuts Beach Grill**, outside Dewey, toward Playa Flamenco, 742-0517 or 742-0280
True to Culebra style, this restaurant has a relaxed feel. Although the cuisine is not fancy by any means, the location makes this a prime eating spot. Burgers and seafood are most popular, but it's the beachside location that draws us in.

$$$ **Dinghy Dock**, on the road to Ensenada Honda in Dewey, 742-0233
Culebra's most popular restaurant for breakfast and dinner sits on the water and features grilled local seafood (lobster, grouper, yellowtail, and tuna). Its hearty pasta plates are a tasty cheap option. Open Monday through Wednesday, 11:30 a.m. to 12:30 p.m. for lunch and 6:30 to 9 p.m. for dinner; open Thursday through Sunday, 8:30 a.m. to 11:30 p.m.

$ **El Batey**, on the airport road by the baseball field, 742-3828
    Culebrenses rave about El Batey's sandwiches. Open from 8
    a.m. to 2 p.m., it also opens later for drinks and dancing.

$ **El Caobo (Tina's)**, Barriada Clark, 742-0505
    In the neighborhood between Dewey and the airport, this
    small, funky place serves good, cheap Puerto Rican cuisine.
    Open daily.

$$ **Heather's Pizzeria**, 14 Calle Pedro Marquez, Dewey, 742-3175
    Heather's is a cool spot for folks to quench their pizza crav-
    ings. It serves good sandwiches and salads, too. People also
    enjoy the happy hour at this well-run establishment.

$ **La Pista**, at the Culebra airport, 742-0166
    The owner of the once popular former Culebra Deli has
    opened another simple restaurant-cafeteria serving *criollo*
    food. However, this eatery has a much better location — in
    front of the Culebra airport, rather than behind the post of-
    fice. This is a great place for breakfast or lunch. It is well
    known for its chicken plates and its *empanadillas*. Open Mon-
    day to Friday, 5:30 a.m. to 2 p.m.; Saturday and Sunday, 7:30
    a.m. to 2 p.m.

$$$ **Mamacita's**, 66 Calle Castelar, Dewey, 742-0322
    This colorful and pleasant patio by the canal is the setting for
    affordable lunch and dinner (and Ben & Jerry's ice cream).
    It's also a great place for a cocktail. Open 10:30 a.m. to 4 p.m.
    for lunch ($$) and 6 to 9 p.m. for dinner. Reservations are
    suggested on weekends.

$$ **White Sands**, in Club Seabourne, Calle Fulladoza, 742-3169
    Just past Bayview Villas overlooking the Ensenada Honda is
    this jewel of a restaurant, located in the wonderful Club Sea-
    bourne. Chef Nicolas cooks up creative *nuevo latino* and Carib-
    bean cuisine. With tables out on the porch, this is a great place
    for dinner or happy hour. Don't miss the award-winning duck
    patacón.

Going Out

Culebra certainly isn't Ibiza, but nightlife on the island has slowly improved. Faced with the challenging task, we have compiled the best places — actually, the only places!

El Batey, 742-3828

Though a restaurant by day, El Batey turns into a late-night Culebra spot (which around here is not so late). It's not South Beach, by any means, but dancing definitely ensues when the DJ spins mostly Latin tunes. Drinks are cheap, especially during happy hour.

Happy Landing

For those who can't decide if they want to party or go to the airport, Happy Landing is the perfect match. Yes, it is located at the end of the airstrip, thus the clever name. A relaxed air pervades here, as cheap beer and pool tables dominate (no food is served). Beware of stumbling pilots (hopefully post-flight!).

Heather's Pizzeria, 14 Calle Pedro Marquez, Dewey, 742-3175

This centrally located hangout offers cheap drinks and tasty pizza. Mixed with super-friendly staff and a lively happy hour, it's no wonder so many seem to pass the time here.

Mamacita's, 742-0322

Though not open very late, Mamacita's has live drummers and attracts people for its happy-hour specials. It also has some great original cocktails (and one of the best T-shirts in the area!).

DON'T MISS

Paradise Gift Shop

A great place for groovy souvies, this shop, located right next to Mamacita's on Calle Castelar in Dewey (742-3569), is a must stop. Open daily from 9 a.m. to 2 p.m. and 5 to 8 p.m.

Isla de Culebra Tourist Guide
For $2.50, this is a good thing to buy when you arrive. It's available at most shops, including Paradise.

La Loma Gift Shop
Owned by Bruce and Kathie Goble, creators of the Culebra Island Web site, www.culebra-island.com, this shop is located in downtown Dewey just steps from the bridge leading to the fire station. Bruce and Kathie are a wealth of information on the island. You can also pick up a copy of the *Isla de Culebra Tourist Guide* at their store.

The Culebra Calendar
This local monthly newspaper is a good source of Culebra happenings.

Water Sports
All these beautiful beaches (and no streams or rivers to cloud the water) — get thee out on them! For ✪scuba diving (depths range up to 100 feet, and the reefs are in great shape), call the Culebra Dive Shop (787-507-4656), Culebra Divers (787-742-0566), or Spa Ventures (787-742-0581). We have gotten positive feedback about a new dive shop that recently opened called Aquatic Adventures (209-3494), run by Captain Taz Hamrick, former military man. Anglers should contact Flamenco Fishing (787-742-3144). Kayaks can be rented at Villa Boheme.

Vieques

W illiam (*never* Bill) is one of our know-it-all friends. At a recent cocktail party we overheard him holding court about how he's read that Vieques is fast becoming the new *it* destination in the Caribbean. More people are *reading* and *talking* about Vieques, and it is now one of those "secrets" that everybody knows about. The good news is that not nearly as many of the people who are reading and talking about Vieques are actually *going* there. In other words, although this beach-studded island has experienced a boom in recent years — well, at least in Vieques terms — it is far from being overrun with tourists. Of course there are many more visitors these days, which has resulted in more specialized hotels and restaurants springing up. However, these small changes are no cause for panic — the island is still as charming as ever.

One of the Spanish Virgin Islands, Vieques lies 7 miles east of Puerto Rico and is considered a municipality within the Commonwealth of Puerto Rico. Viequenses, as the almost 10,000 residents are called, are also U.S. citizens. About two-thirds of the island was owned by the U.S. Navy, which for nearly 60 years used the island for live bombing practice (this means real bombs). Military maneuvers were

Vieques

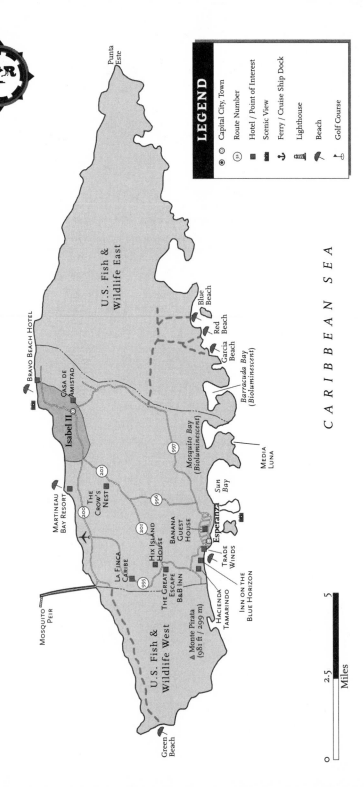

N

ATLANTIC OCEAN

CARIBBEAN SEA

Punta Este

U.S. Fish & Wildlife East

Bravo Beach Hotel

Casa de Amistad

Isabel II

Blue Beach

Red Beach

Garcia Beach

Barracuda Bay (Bioluminescent)

Mosquito Bay (Bioluminescent)

Media Luna

Martineau Bay Resort

The Crow's Nest

201

200

Sun Bay

996

Esperanza

Trade Winds

Banana Guest House

Hix Island House

203

La Finca Caribe

The Great Escape B&B Inn

Hacienda Tamarindo

Inn on the Blue Horizon

995

Mosquito Peir

▲ Monte Pirata (981 ft / 299 m)

U.S. Fish & Wildlife West

Green Beach

997

0   2.5   5

Miles

executed from the huge Roosevelt Roads Naval Station, on the other side of the Pasaje de Vieques in Puerto Rico. Even napalm was dropped on the island. The military presence, and particularly the continued live bombing, infuriated many locals (it would us, too!) because it upset the wonderful ambiance of the island. Who wants to live in a bombing range? Tensions heightened in April 1999, when a civilian was killed and four were injured by two stray 500-pound bombs. This incident made the U.S. military presence a hot-button issue, not only in Vieques but in all of Puerto Rico. After the bombing accident, President Clinton commissioned a study to determine the need (or lack thereof) for a continued U.S. military presence in Vieques and Puerto Rico. This, combined with massive local protests and negative international media attention, finally resulted in the Navy relinquishing control of its former base on the west end of the island in May 2001. By May 2003, the Navy gave up control of its remaining base on the east end of the island and ceased bombing completely. With its departure, the Navy returned about 25,000 acres of land to Vieques. Although the land is still in need of a major cleanup effort, much of it has been made available for local housing and other development. An even greater portion of the acreage is preserved as conservation land administered by the U.S. Fish and Wildlife Service and the Puerto Rican Conservation Trust. These conservation lands, including the island's popular beaches, are now open to the public.

There are two towns on Vieques: **Isabel II** on the north side, the island's port and commercial center, and **Esperanza**, a smaller, mellower town on the south side geared more toward tourism. Of a total of about 55 square miles, only 17 are available for residential and commercial use. Even so, this part of Vieques seems uncrowded, unspoiled (no mega-resorts, fast-food chains, or traffic lights), and often very pretty. The island is hilly but lacks the big peaks to capture rain clouds (the highest summit is Mt. Pirata, at 981 feet). Hence it is an arid island (about 40 inches of rainfall annually) and a marked contrast to the El Yunque rainforest, just 16 miles away in Puerto Rico. Vegetation here is similar to other Caribbean islands like Antigua and many of the Grenadines. Fortunately, water is piped in from the El Yunque watershed, so shower water pressure is good.

After a few days on the island, we noticed that an inordinate number of New Englanders, especially from Massachusetts and particularly

Vieques: Key Facts

Location	18°N by 65°W 7 miles east of Puerto Rico 1,660 miles southeast of New York
Size	55 square miles 21 miles long by 5 miles wide
Highest point	Mt. Pirata (981 feet)
Population	Approximately 10,000
Language	Spanish (but most Viequenses speak English)
Time	Atlantic Standard Time (1 hour ahead of EST, same as EDT)
Area code	787 (must be dialed before all local numbers as well)
Electricity	110 volts AC, 60 cycles, same as U.S. and Canada
Currency	The U.S. dollar
Driving	On the right
Documents	None for Americans and no Customs hassles, either. Canadians need a passport if traveling by air, or proof of nationality (birth certificate, certificate of citizenship and government-issued photo ID) if arriving by sea. By January 2008, Canadians will need a passport even if traveling by sea. Brits need a visa unless they hold an e-passport or a passport conforming to certain other specific U.S. government requirements. (Check with the U.S. Consulate or your travel agent for more specifics.)
Departure tax	None
Beer to drink	Medalla
Rum to drink	Don Q or Bacardi
Music to hear	Reggae, rock, and *reggaetón*
Tourism info	787-741-0800 www.vieques-island.com www.enchanted-isle.com www.viequestourism.com

the Boston area, have moved here. Perhaps the no-frills air of Vieques appeals to our Yankee mentality, or maybe it was just that real estate was cheap. (Prices have risen considerably but are still cheaper than on many other islands.) We also noticed that besides some outdoor activities like going to the beach, reading, exploring the island, and maybe diving or snorkeling, there's not a helluva lot to do here. It's fine if that is your intention. Another thing we noticed (we're so observant) is that very few of the lodging options are on a swimmable beach. It is necessary to rent a car and drive. This might be an inconvenience for some. Finally, we noticed a lot of couples, which makes sense given the paucity of nightlife. It's definitely B.Y.O.B. (Bring Your Own Bedmate).

The Briefest History

The Taíno (Arawak) Indians first settled the island about 2500 B.C. and prospered until the arrival of Columbus in 1493. He named the island Vieques after its Taíno name Bieques ("Small Island") and claimed it for Spain. A series of rebellions and disease epidemics ensued, and by 1514 the Taínos were gone from the island, either enslaved in Puerto Rico or dead. Between 1514 and 1843, the island remained uninhabited and under the control of Spain's command post in Puerto Rico. As happened with most Caribbean islands, the European powers all tried to get their hands on it. Colonization attempts were made by the English, Danish, and French, and all were repelled by the Spanish forces in Puerto Rico. During this period of skirmishes over Vieques, many pirates, sustained by seafood, shellfish, and fowl, called the island home.

Annoyed with other nations trying to capture the flag of Vieques, Spain finally made the island a Spanish municipality in 1843, and a fort was built and a colony begun. Prosperity followed in the form of sugar plantations worked by African slaves brought over from neighboring English islands (slavery was abolished in the English colonies in 1834 but not in Puerto Rico until 1873). In 1898 the Spanish-American War ceded the island to the United States, which absorbed Vieques into the Commonwealth of Puerto Rico. At that time there were four *centrales* ("sugar mills") in operation, owned by just a few families who didn't share their wealth. Worker conditions were deplorable and remained so until a general strike in 1915 improved the workers' situation significantly. Sugar and fishing sustained the island's economy until World War II.

With American involvement in the war inevitable, the U.S. Navy initiated a search for a training and maneuvers area that would be similar to the climate and conditions of the Japanese-occupied South Pacific. They found it on the east coast of Puerto Rico (Roosevelt Roads) and on Vieques. In 1941, 70 percent of Vieques was expropriated, much to the chagrin of its 10,000-plus residents. The Navy land grab shut down the *centrales* (the last one closed in 1942). Construction jobs for the bases provided employment for a few years, but by 1945, about 3,000 Viequenses had been relocated to St. Croix. The rest were left in the middle section of the island with few or no employment opportunities. Thus the seeds of the anti-Navy movement were sown. The live bombing and use of other lethal weapons on the island from World War II onward accelerated the momentum. With the April 1999 incident, when a civilian was killed by a stray bomb, that movement gained momentum and was fueled by public outrage. This ultimately resulted in the full withdrawal of U.S. military forces in May 2003.

While many Viequenses sought economic opportunity in Puerto Rico or the United States, the Puerto Rican government tried and failed several times to reestablish agriculture. Finally realizing that that wasn't the way to go, it shifted the emphasis toward industry in the 1960s. With the added boost of Federal Tax Code 936, which gave U.S. companies huge tax breaks if they invested in and established plants or companies in Puerto Rico, the economic picture brightened in Vieques. The 1969 opening of the General Electric plant anchored the effort; it is still in operation today. Tourism on the island is a relatively recent phenomenon. In its infancy in the 1980s, tourism accelerated into the 1990s as Vieques was discovered by both independent travelers and the media.

Getting There

The most convenient way to get to Vieques is to fly from San Juan's Luis Muñoz Marín International Airport. Vieques Air Link (www .vieques-island.com/val, 888-901-9247, stateside, 787-741-8331 in

Isla Verde and San Juan) has three round-trip flights daily to Vieques's fairly new, modern terminal. Round-trip airfare is $167 for adults and children. Planes are of the small propeller variety, so early reservations are advised. The trip takes about 30 minutes. Vieques Air Link also offers several daily flights from the smaller, domestic Isla Grande Airport (located just to the west of the Miramar section of San Juan), which is very convenient for anyone staying in Old San Juan or the Condado. Isla Nena Air Service (www.islanena.8m.com; 877-812-5144 stateside, 787-863-3075 in San Juan) also flies to Vieques from Marín International Airport. In addition, Vieques Air Link has scheduled service from San Juan's smaller, domestic Isla Grande Airport (just to the west of the Miramar section of San Juan and very convenient for anyone staying in the Condado or Old San Juan). Both airlines offer charter service. Air Flamenco (www.airflamenco .net, 787-724-1818) also offers flights from Isla Grande Airport. Another charter option is Air America (www.airamericacaribbean.com, 787-276-5669), which offers one-way, five-person flights for $450 or nine-person flights for $900. Finally, a new American Eagle terminal is under construction, and the expectation is that by November 2007 it will be running scheduled flights from Luis Muñoz to Vieques.

Another option is to fly from Fajardo, which is an hour to an hour and a half east of San Juan (depending on traffic). This small airport has a lot more daily flights, and they take only 10 minutes. Both Vieques Air Link and Isla Nena Air Service offer scheduled and charter service here. Finding the airport is a tad tricky, so pay attention to the airport signs and don't be afraid to ask for directions (it happens often here).

The **Fajardo Port Authority** provides passenger and car ferry service three times daily to Vieques (787-863-0705 in Fajardo and 787-741-4761 in Vieques). Passengers do not need reservations; the fare is $4 round-trip. Reservations are necessary for cars; fares are $26 round-trip for the car plus $4 for each passenger. The trip takes an hour.

Finally, there is a seasonal Fast Ferry service available from Old San Juan to Vieques that takes under two hours. The one-way cost is $47; the round-trip fare is $73. Contact Island Hi-Speed Ferry at 877-899-3993 or www.islandhispeedferry.com more information.

Getting Around

Since you have to drive to get to a swimming beach in Vieques (especially a good one), renting a car is a must. Although the island roads are in good shape and are well marked, the naval base roads can get bumpy. We suggest renting a jeep for this reason—and because it's fun. Be sure to request one with a removable soft top (even more fun). Rentals range between $35 and $50 a day for jeeps and cars. Minivans are about $60. Although there was discussion at press time of a Hertz opening up, all current rental companies are local, and most will arrange for airport pickup and drop-off (or will let you leave the car at the airport). Our favorite is Maritza's Car Rentals (787-741-0078); it features great vehicles, such as soft-top 4 × 4 Jeeps, and it offers drop-off service to hotels. Or try Island Car Rentals (787-741-1666; islandcar@aol.com) or Steve's Car Rentals (787-741-8135). For moto rental, try **Extreme Scooter Rental** (787-435-2121)—its scooters are about $55 per day.

Focus on Vieques:
Mellowing Out on the Beaches

We know that's a very '70s expression—"mellow out"—and we really have tried to erase that decade from our collective memory, but the term is really what Vieques is all about. How does one mellow out? Well, just staying here will automatically start you on the path. Reading, sleeping, and maybe a few cocktails will help. Lying or walking on the beach and swimming in the clear turquoise water won't hurt, either.

There are a lot of undeveloped beaches to explore. Although Vieques lacks the truly stunning beaches of its sister Culebra, or of St. John or Anguilla, most visitors will be very pleased with the more than 50 options available (we're more than a little jaded, so it takes a lot to impress us). Our favorite are Sun Bay, Media Luna, and Navio Beach. All hotels provide directions to the island's beaches, which, with one exception (Green Beach), are on the south side of the island.

Sun Bay is just east of the center of Esperanza and wins the prize for best beach on Vieques. A long, palm-fringed crescent of white sand with good swimming areas (many of the island's beaches have shallow coral reefs close to the water's edge), Sun Bay also has picnic tables, bathroom facilities, and a sandy road that runs parallel to it. The best part is on the left (eastern) end of the beach, where it's calmer and there is good snorkeling. The beach is "open" from 7 a.m. until 5 p.m. and requires a $2 parking fee; call 787-741-8198 for more information. Media Luna and Navio Beach are accessed from the bumpy, sandy road at Sun Bay. **Media Luna** is fairly secluded and has shade trees, shallow calm water, and good snorkeling (again on the eastern side). **Navio Beach** is small, very secluded, and framed by rocky bluffs; it is only a half-hour walk from Sun Bay, has the most-turquoise water, and often has body-surfable waves. Some bathers take it all off here. Be advised that there is no shade, so bring an umbrella.

On the east end of the island is **Camp García**. Here, on the south coast, are Red, Blue, and García Beaches, which are now all open to the public.

Also on the east end is **Green Beach**. This faces Puerto Rico and has great views of El Yunque. However, stick to weekdays here; on weekends boaters from Fajardo anchor at Green Beach, and it gets crowded. Sheltered from the trade winds, the beach can get buggy by mid-afternoon if it has rained recently. Blue and Red Beaches have become popular spots now that the military base is closed. They are easily accessed by road—a taxi from Esperanza runs about $10.

Where to Stay

We were surprised to see that the level of sophistication has risen here in the past few years; more swanky inns and fine restaurants are popping up on this little island. Our new favorite hotel on the island, Bravo Beach Hotel, is one prime example. Also, in 2008, the W plans to make its first appearance here. At press time, the W was undergoing an $18-million renovation of the temporarily closed Martineau Bay Resort. It should reopen in September 2008 as the world's first W Resort—the W Martineau Bay Resort. Although we're not fans of the idea of large-scale resorts on Vieques, the expectation is that the W will at least enhance the style of this 156-room property, which, though attractive, could use a little more character. (For more information and updates on this project, visit www.starwoodhotels.com/martineua or call 787-741-4100.) Fortunately, for those seeking the small and serene, have no worries—the island is still a place of tiny inns, guesthouses, and villa rentals (although we were disappointed to learn that Casa Cielo, and its beautiful sweeping views, is no longer a guesthouse but has become a private residence).

⊛ **Bravo Beach Hotel**, P.O. Box 1374, North Shore Road, Vieques, PR. ℂ 787-741-1128, ✎ 787-741-3918, 🖳 www.bravobeachhotel.com

💲 **Very Pricey** 🍴 **BP** ꜀꜀ 9 rooms, plus a 2-bedroom villa

This sensual oceanside boutique hotel takes accommodation in Vieques to a whole new level. Owned by a trio of fashion-minded New Yorkers who transformed an old hacienda into an ultra-stylish hotel, Bravo retains some tradition in its architecture, most specifically in the design of its central plaza and fountain and in the restaurant that is shaped like a passing ship. However, the rooms evoke a much more modern appeal. Everything here is done to the max. The rooms are super-modern, with white throughout and sleek glass doors opening onto private lanais. The queen-size mahogany beds are draped with gauzy mosquito nets and outfitted with Frette linens, and the bathrooms are stocked with Aveda bath products. All rooms come equipped with satellite TV, DVD players, iPod docking stations (way cool!), and Playstations for rainy days. Original art and photography adorn the rooms, which also have ceiling fans, a/c, and dehumidifiers. Our favorite rooms are 3 through 7, which are oceanfront studios with the best views. Although there are only 11 rooms, there are two pools for guests to enjoy, one right over the ocean and the other in the garden, replete with cushions and an honor bar. An upstairs sea-view deck is perfect for special events and massages. Hanging at the new poolside Palms Lounge with its red lights and chill tunes would be our ideal "night out." After one night here, we were seduced by the comfortable style of Bravo and were not surprised to learn of the accolades this boutique hotel is quickly garnering. Here's another: the renowned Rum & Reggae Sexiest Hotel in Puerto Rico Award.

⊛ **Hacienda Tamarindo**, P.O. Box 1569, Route 996, km 4.5, Vieques, PR. ⓒ 787-741-0420, ✆ 787-741-3215, 🖳 www.haciendatamarindo.com, hactam@aol.com

💲 **Pricey** and up ⑪ **BP** CC 16 rooms

We adore the Hacienda Tamarindo, a Spanish-style inn opened in 1997, set on breezy rising grounds with sweeping views of sloping pastures and the Caribbean. Ex-Vermonters Linda and Burr Vail built and opened the inn in an amazingly short time, considering the difficulties of building and running a business in the Caribbean and on a small island. With it they've created an extraordinarily comfortable and warm environment. They are a very amiable and hospitable couple, and their friendly and helpful style as innkeepers is one of the great things about the Hacienda. So is the 40-something-foot tamarind tree growing smack dab in the middle of the inn (it graces the Hacienda's atrium and dining terrace). The Vails' collection of art, collectibles, and antiques acquired during years in Vermont adorn both the public spaces and the guest rooms. An honor bar in the lobby provides refreshment, and there is an air-conditioned lounge with TV-VCR and a library. Outside, at a pretty pool with chaises, you can take a dip and get some sun. Be sure to say hello to the talking parrot. He'll give you an earful!

Each of the rooms has its own style and décor (Linda was a commercial interior designer), and all feature mahogany louvered doors and windows, terra-cotta tile floors, ceiling fans, and baths with tile showers. A suite comes with a Jacuzzi tub and private lanai. The Hacienda is also wheelchair accessible. A full American breakfast is served on the second-floor dining terrace (we loved the real Vermont maple syrup on the table). We hope the new condos being built by the hotel's owners don't compromise the intimate setting here, but we are confident that the Hacienda will retain its tranquillity, because these units will be located slightly down the hill.

No children under 15 are allowed (that means no screaming kids and stroller obstacles — we like that!).

⊛ **Inn on the Blue Horizon**, P.O. Box 1556, Route 996, km 4.5,
Vieques, PR. ℭ 787-741-3318 or 787-741-0527,
✆ 787-741-0522, ▣ www.innonthebluehorizon.com,
info@innonthebluehorizon.com

💰 **Very Pricey** and up 🍽 **CP** ⒸⒸ 10 rooms

The first time we visited the Inn on the Blue Horizon in
1996, there were only three rooms, and Café Blu was the island's best restaurant. Now there are 10 rooms at this wonderful place, and the restaurant was reopened (on Valentine's
Day — how perfect!) after a kitchen fire. The inn, set on 20
acres, is under new ownership but is still beautifully decorated — to within an inch of its life. Common areas have big
overstuffed sofas and chairs; antiques, art, and open space
abound. Books and magazines are placed just so, and dramatic flower arrangements are strategically located throughout the inn. It's like a page out of *Architectural Digest*. There
is a library crammed with books. A pretty pool surrounded by
a tile deck faces the sea and is bordered by a hibiscus hedge.
There are even two tennis courts and a tiny gym for the gym
bunnies among us. With all this studied stylishness comes a
slight attitude, but since we can give it, too (only when de-
served, of course), it didn't bother us a bit.

Not surprisingly, the guest rooms (a few in the main
house and the rest sharing three cottages) are extremely tasteful. Most have four-poster beds; all rooms have queen- or
king-size beds, except one, which has an antique double four-
poster. All rooms except for the suite in the main house are
air-conditioned and are also cooled by the steady trade winds
and ceiling fans. All have antiques, terra-cotta tile floors, a
color scheme of warm muted tones, bright upholstery and
fabrics, all-cotton linens, cut flowers, glass-block showers, and
spacious lanais with white wooden chairs (in the cottage
units). Our favorite rooms are called Mariana and Esperanza.
The Joseph and Judith rooms in the back cottage, though very

pretty, did not have as good a view of the sea as the other cottage rooms. The original three main-house rooms have high ceilings, four-poster beds, and very dramatic drapes. Thoughtful touches in the rooms include a beach umbrella and chairs, a cooler and thermos, beach towels, a flashlight, and bug spray.

There has been discussion that this stylish inn will be adding another 40 or so rooms in the near future, but no date has been set for this expansion, nor is anybody sure if it will even happen. We're happy with the way things are.

No children under 14 are allowed during high season.

The Crow's Nest, P.O. Box 1521, Route 201, km 1.6, Vieques, PR. ℭ 877-CROWS-NEST or 787-741-0033, ✆ 787-741-1294, ▱ www.crowsnestvieques.com, thenest@coqui.net

▣ **Cheap** ⑪ **CP** ⓒⓒ 17 units

This is the epitome of what Vieques used to be; very casual, no-frill, laid-back, and inexpensive. Seven of the Crow's Nest's units are rented as condos, and 10 as hotel rooms — which are actually condos rented out by the inn. With new owners Scott Bowie and Eli Belendez, this 5-acre inland property sits on a hillside with sweeping views to the north of Vieques Sound and Culebra. The units, all freshly painted, are studios with TVs, kitchenettes, phones, ceiling fans, a/c, coolers, and beach towels and chairs. Some units have a balcony or private terrace. Best of all, it won't break the bank to stay here. The Crow's Nest boasts one of Vieques's best restaurants, Island Steakhouse, and a friendly bar, too. Although the Island Steakhouse is now open only on Tuesday for an all-you-can-eat barbecue, the slack has been taken up by the property's new restaurant, El Jardin. There is a comfortable pool and a lounge area as well.

No children under 12 are allowed from May through mid-November.

The Great Escape B&B Inn, Box 14501, HC-02, Vieques, PR. ℭ 787-741-2927 or 787-736-4927, ▱ www.enchanted-isle .com/greatescape, jonssch@coqui.net

▣ **Not So Cheap** ⑪ **CP** ⓒⓒ 10 rooms, plus 1 two- or three-room apartment

Nestled up in the hills is this remote bed & breakfast, ideal for those who want a time-out from flashy hotels and big crowds. Although it's quite a distance from the beach and most rooms are devoid of sea views, the house is located on a spacious plot of open land with pleasant green views. The rooms are housed in a two-story house, and each has a vista of the hills. Activity is centered around the tile pool deck, which has an honor bar with some chairs in the sun and others under shelter for those sunburn victims. We like that there is a stereo for guests to use, as well as comfy chairs and a little cactus garden with figurines. Hammocks add a pleasant touch. All of the well-ventilated rooms have poster beds and ceiling fans, but at press time, only one had a/c. Sure, it's a bit out of the way and best for those with a rental car, but as the name indicates, it's a Great Escape. The funky mirrored Mickey Mouse outhouse near the pool is most unusual!

Casa de Amistad, 27 Benitez Castaño, Vieques, PR. ✆ 787-741-3758, 🖳 www.casadeamistad.com, viequesamistad@aol.com

💲 **Cheap** 🍴 **EP** ⒸⒸ 7 rooms

This cozy guesthouse is a great place to unwind. The rooms are simple but equipped with a/c, ceiling fan, and minibar. What we like most about the "Friendship House" is the intimacy. We felt very comfortable staying here, and we found plenty of hangout spots, from the wicker furniture on the front porch to the library with satellite TV, to the "freshwater" plunge pool and the garden in the backyard. The honor bar in the lobby is a nice addition, especially for those sitting by the pool or in the library. The rooftop deck is an added bonus and so is the guest computer and the Wi-Fi access in the café. The guesthouse is not right on the ocean, but for those who desire a seaside accommodation, it is also possible to rent out the Becker Room, two blocks away, which looks right over the sea.

⭐ **La Finca Caribe**, P.O. Box 1332, Route 995, km 2.5, Vieques, PR. ✆ 787-741-0495, 🖂 787-741-3584, 🖳 www.lafinca.com, manager@lafinca.com

💼 **Cheap** and up 🍽 **EP** CC 1 six-room house and 2 cottages

Formerly the very funky women's retreat known as New Dawn, the eco-friendly La Finca Caribe is definitely a different kind of lodging experience. Though no longer just a women's retreat, La Finca is still funky. Think Indian print bedspreads, summer camp, Birkenstocks, pajama parties, rustic communal living, hammocks, and the music of Jimmy Buffet all rolled into one, and you have an image of what this place is like. With the addition of some paint and a much-needed swimming pool (curiously salt water despite the fact that La Finca is way up in the hills and 3 miles from the beach), it's certainly in better shape than the New Dawn ever was. However, if you have an aversion to plywood, you won't like it here — the exterior and the floors are just that. Nevertheless, there is a good-size porch with hammocks, and all showers are outdoors (and enclosed, of course).

The six rooms in the main house share two baths. All have mosquito nets, white walls and whitewashed floors, wall hangings, Indian print upholstery, and not a lot of privacy. There are two separate cabañas: one with a separate bedroom and private bath and the other a studio with sleeping loft. There are no TVs or phones in the rooms and cabañas. There is a communal kitchen in the main house. The entire place can be rented to a group and claims to sleep up to 27 (soon-to-be close friends) people.

Hix Island House, P.O. Box 14902, HC-02, Vieques, PR. 📞 787-741-2302, ✎ 787-741-2797, 🖥 www.hixislandhouse.com, info@hixislandhouse.com

💼 **Wicked Pricey** 🍽 **CP** CC 13 rooms

This ultra-modern spot may be featured in architectural and fashion magazines and has won multiple environmental awards, but we didn't enjoy our stay here. The inn is the creation of Canadian architect John Hix, who has created a stunning concrete collection of loft apartments in the middle of the forest. Yes, indeed, it is definitely a strange mix. We aren't turned off by the idea of super-mod design in the woods—in fact, we love that style. Our gripe is that as guests, we just weren't very comfortable. Perhaps the biggest problem is the fact the inn is located high in the woods, without sweeping vistas (except one at the pool). In these parts, this means that there are a lot of mosquitoes, which become quite a pain when the rooms have no screens. The beds have mosquito nets, but we have heard some guests complain that they don't always offer sufficient protection. The rooms are ultra-minimalist, with rough unfinished concrete, which might be great for a gallery in Berlin, but it just doesn't work for us in a tropical setting like Vieques. To be honest, the gray concrete makes the whole place look unfinished. Each apartment has a veranda and full kitchen. If we have to choose, Room 1 is our favorite, although the Matisse Room has a great rooftop deck. One feature we do really like (and wish was more common) is that the inn stocks the refrigerators with fresh bread, fruit, and juice, so guests can make breakfast at their leisure. Oh, and of course, we love the open-air showers. We must admit that the pool design is divine. No children under 12 are allowed. Yoga is offered three days a week.

Trade Winds Guest House and Restaurant, P.O. Box 1012, 107 Calle Flamboyan, Malecón, Esperanza, Vieques, PR.
℡ 787-741-8666, ✎ 787-741-2964, 🖳 www.enchanted-isle .com/tradewinds, tradewns@coqui.net

💲 Cheap 🍴 EP 🆑 11 rooms

Located right in Esperanza on the western end of the Malecón, this is a fairly modern, motelish lodging with an affordable price tag and a convenient location. Its shortage of ambiance and direct location on the Malecón make it a less desirable place to stay. However, the open-air restaurant has good ocean views, and the newly renovated rooms are an enhancement since our last visit. All rooms include private bath and ceiling fans. Some rooms also have a/c, kitchenettes, and lanais.

Villa Rentals

For groups or families, a villa rental is probably your best bet, and there is a good selection from which to choose. These reputable companies can find the right place for you and can help with other island details as well.

Connections/Jane Sabin Real Estate, P.O. Box 358, 117 Calle Munoz Rivera, Vieques, PR. ✆ 787-741-0023, ✉ 787-741-2022, 🖳 www.enchanted-isle.com/connections

Crow's Nest Realty, P.O. Box 1409, Vieques, PR. ✆ 787-741-3298 or 787-741-0033, ✉ 787-741-1294, 🖳 www.crowsnestrealty .com, sheilevin@aol.com, elibelendez@yahoo.com

Rainbow Realty, 278 Calle Flamboyan, Esperanza, Vieques, PR. Contact Lin Wetherby. Known for being gay-friendly, but as Lin also says, "We are straight-friendly!" ✆ 787-741-4312 or 787-741-5068, 🖳 www.enchanted-isle.com/rainbow, rainbowrealty@hotmail.com

Where to Eat

For such a small place, there are a surprisingly large number of restaurants. Here are our picks.

$$ **Bananas**, Calle Flamboyan, Malecón, Esperanza, 741-8700
This fun, casual open-air restaurant (of course there's a roof) is a local gathering spot and a great place to hang out and work on some margaritas. It looks out on the Malecón and the sea beyond. The menu is pub fare: steaks, grilled seafood, and its famous burgers. Open daily for lunch and dinner until 10 or 11 p.m. (depending on business).

$$$ **Bilí**, 144 Flamboyan, Malecón, Esperanza, 741-1382
This well-designed restaurant (in the Amapola Inn) right on the Malecón is a little pricey but tasty. We love the coco martinis and also recommend the rigatoni with crabmeat ragu. Open Wednesday through Sunday for lunch and dinner.

$$$ **Café Media Luna**, 351 A. G. Mellado, Isabel II, 741-2594
Located in downtown Isabel II, this restaurant in a restored
house offers a creative international menu by chef Monica
Chitnis. The café is one of Vieques cultural meccas, so keep
an eye open for live music. Open Wednesday to Sunday, 7 to
10:30 p.m. in season; off-season Friday through Sunday.

$$$ **Chez Shack**, Route 995, km 8.6, 741-2175
This funky collection of brightly painted tin shacks was orig-
inally built around 1910. Just down the road from La Finca
Caribe, Chez Shack offers a great menu of local dishes and
seafood and has a very popular barbecue on Monday night—
a mesquite grill featuring lobster, shrimp, steak, lamb, and
fish, along with a salad bar. Eat in the sun or in the shade.
Open daily, 6 to 11 p.m. or so.

$$$ **Island Steakhouse**, Route 201, km 1.6, 741-0011
The popular restaurant at the Crow's Nest has made a few
changes. Hurricane Georges took off the restaurant's back
roof, which has been replaced, and a new open deck has been
added to the front. The new chefs have done a great job. They
do lunch during the high season as well. Happy hour is from
5 to 7 p.m. Note that the plan for fall 2007 is for this restau-
rant to be open only on Tuesday for a $22/person, all-you-can-
eat barbecue. (As a result of this new schedule, folks are now
spending time at The Crow's Nest's new restaurant, El Jardin,
which serves a variety of Caribbean and American cuisine.)

$$$ **M Bar**, Isabel II, 741-4000
The anticipated second restaurant of Puerto Rican chef Juan
Camacho should now be open here in Isabel II next to Uva.
His nouvelle cuisine places an emphasis on the freshest in-
gredients. The style of the restaurant, with its raw wood and
cement, adds to the ambiance. Look right into the kitchen
and watch him do his thing.

$$ **Trade Winds**, 107 Flamboyan, Malecón, Esperanza, 741-8666
We simply love this seaside restaurant that is elevated to take
in the fresh breezes. There is a varied array of cuisine options,

but all are consistently delicious. The Caribbean fish cakes are a popular starter, but we favor the warmed goat cheese with sun-dried tomatoes and crostini. For those not ready for pricey lobster, try the guava chicken with sherry-guava glaze or the Thai coco-curry pasta with shrimp. Open Friday through Tuesday for breakfast (homemade corned beef hash is a favorite) and lunch, and daily for dinner.

$$$ **Uva**, 359 Calle Antonio Mellado, Isabel II, 741-2050
This stylish rustic eatery is a member of the latest generation of upscale restaurants to hit Vieques in recent years. The Argentine chef offers a range of specialties, from meats to pasta. Cool tunes pervade throughout, and the bar is a great place to relax with a drink. Open from 7 to 10:30 p.m.; closed Tuesday.

Going Out

Not quite a nocturnal mecca, Vieques is still more of a day-lover's place. But some of the restaurants along the Malecón (such as Bananas, Bilí, and Trade Winds) and in Isabel II (Uva and M Bar) are great places to relax at night.

Al's Mar Azul, Calle Plinio Peterson, 741-3400
Located steps from the ferry terminal, this laid-back bar is pure Caribbean. Its outdoor deck offers wonderful sunset views that are well-timed for happy-hour dollar beers. The pool table and darts add activities, and the crowd here runs the whole Vieques spectrum. Closed on Tuesday during the low season.

The Palms, Isabel II, 741-1128
The Palms is a part of the Bravo Beach Hotel — in fact, it's the second pool, which the hotel opens to the public on weekend nights. We love sitting along the red-lit pool here, enjoying a cocktail as the DJ spins loungelike house music. There are cushions laid out along the edge of the elevated pool, which is in tune with the easygoing sexy vibe. This is a very romantic setting and an ideal spot for a late-night swim, so dress accordingly. Open weekends until late.

DON'T MISS

Bioluminescent Bays

Mosquito and Barracuda are two of the few bioluminescent bays in the world. There was also one in La Parguera, Puerto Rico, but failure to protect its fragile ecosystem led to a fading of its bioluminescence. In the dark of a calm night, phosphorescent plankton (dinoflagellates, to be precise) create "sparks" with any vigorous movement in the water that disturbs their nesting. Island Adventures (787-741-0720, www.biobay.com), which is recently under new ownership, offers popular tours of the bay. The one-and-a-half-hour tour on the pontoon boat includes swimming and stargazing. Departure time is around 6:30 p.m., and rates are about $30 per person. To truly appreciate the serene beauty of the bio bay, we recommend going via kayak. Blue Caribe Kayak (741-2522) is the best bet here.

Snorkeling and Diving

Vieques has some great dive sites and a full-service dive operation. Call the Blue Caribe Dive Center (741-2522) in Esperanza. Captain Richard Barone of Vieques Nature Tours has a glass-bottom boat and offers snorkeling and education tours (787-741-1980). For watersports addicts, Extreme (435-2121) rents jet skis from the Malecón in Esperanza for $100 an hour (yeah, pricey).

Fuerte Conde de Mirasol

The fort in Isabel II was the last to be built by a colonial power in the Western Hemisphere (it was built in the 1840s). It has been restored and now houses interesting island exhibits, art, and the Vieques Historic Archives. Open Wednesday to Sunday from 10 a.m. to 4 p.m. or by special appointment. Call 787-741-1717

SPANISH SURVIVAL GUIDE

Language

One reason that many speakers of English find travel in Puerto Rico so easy is the fact that almost everybody speaks English there. Sure, Spanish is the dominant language, but it's unusual to meet someone involved in tourism who doesn't speak English — and well, too. Still, it's never a bad idea to come armed with a few words of Spanish in the event that you meet that one hot Latino or Latina who just might be impressed with your horrible accent. Also, you never know when you will find yourself faced with a problem in a place that is nowhere near anyone who speaks English.

Generally, Spanish sounds are quite a bit easier than those of French or Portuguese, but in order to avoid doing a total botch job, a quick explanation of pronunciation rules should be helpful. After all, we wouldn't want our readers mispronouncing the two most important words while on a Spanish-speaking vacation. We are, of course, referring to *cerveza*, pronounced "sehr-BEH-sah," or "sehr-VEH-sah," and the ensuing *baño*, pronounced "BAH-nyo." Since we've all heard a fair amount of Spanish, many of the sounds will not be problematic, but here is a short pronunciation key to help with those that are less obvious.

A pronounced "ah" as in "father," not as in "rather"

B like the English *B*, but with less force; when situated between vowels, it has a very soft, almost vibrating sound

C same as in English, with a hard *K* sound before *A*, *O*, and *U*, but a soft sound before *E* and *I*

E like "eh" as in "bed"

G similar to English, except before the letters *E* and *I*, when it has a forceful (almost guttural) *H* sound

H   always silent; just pretend you don't even see this letter

I   pronounced "ee" as in "see"

J   like the English *H*, but with more emphasis (how else would you say José?)

LL   like *Y* as in "yellow"

Ñ   The tilde above the *N* indicates a "ny" sound, as in "onion"

QU   like the English letter *K*

R   slightly rolled in the middle of words; more strongly rolled at the start of words

RR   always heavily rolled (This is where most of us display our horrible accents.)

U   pronounced "oo" as in "boot"

V   In most of South and Central America, this letter is pronounced with the same rules as the letter *B*. So it may often retain a subtler sounding version of the English *V*.

Y   like the English *Y* except when alone, when it sounds like "ee"

Z   Everywhere, except Spain (where it is pronounced like the English "th"), this letter is pronounced like the English *S*.

Greetings and Other Basics

English	Spanish
Hi/Hello.	*Hola.*
Goodbye.	*Adiós.*
See you later.	*Hasta luego.*
What's up?	*¿Qué tal?*
How are you?	*¿Como estás?*
I'm fine.	*Muy bien.*
So-so.	*Así así.*
Please.	*Por favor.*
Thank you.	*Gracias.*
You're welcome.	*De nada.*
Yes.	*Sí.*
No.	*No.*
Good morning.	*Buenos días.*

Good afternoon.	*Buenas tardes.*
Good evening.	*Buenas noches.*
Excuse me.	*Perdóneme.*
I'm sorry.	*Lo siento.*
May I?	*¿Puedo?*
Nice to meet you.	*Mucho gusto.*
Where?	*¿Dónde?*
When?	*¿Cuándo?*
How much?	*¿Cuánto?*
What?	*¿Qué?*
How?	*¿Como?* (Often used as "What?")
Why?	*¿Porqué?*
good	*bueno*
everything/all	*todo*
because	*porque*
for	*por, para*
with	*con*
without	*sin*
thing	*cosa*
My name is...	*Me llamo...*
What is your name?	*¿Como se llama?*
I	*yo*
you	*usted*
he/she	*el/ella*
we	*nosotros*
they (masculine)	*ellos*
they (feminine)	*ellas*

On the Move

Do you speak English?	*¿Entiende el inglés?*
I speak English.	*Yo hablo inglés.*
I don't speak Spanish.	*Yo no hablo español.*
I speak Spanish.	*Yo hablo español.*
How does one say... in Spanish?	*¿Como se dice... en español?*
I want to go to...	*Yo quiero ir a...*
How do I get to...?	*¿Como llego...?*

What is the address?	*¿Cuál es la dirección?*
Where is...?	*¿Dónde está?*
the airplane	*el avion*
the airport	*el aeropuerto*
the bank	*el banco*
the bar	*el bar*
the bathroom	*el baño*
the beach	*la playa*
the boat	*el barco*
the bus	*el bus*
the bus station	*la central camioneta*
the church	*la iglesia*
the currency exchange office	*la casa de cambio*
downtown	*el centro (de la ciudad)*
the drugstore	*la farmacia*
the American Embassy	*la Embajada Norteamericana*
the Australian Embassy	*la Embajada Australiana*
the British Embassy	*la Embajada Británica*
the Canadian Embassy	*la Embajada Canadiense*
the hospital	*el hospital*
the hotel	*el hotel*
the lake	*el lago*
the post office	*el correo*
the restaurant	*el restaurante*
the square	*la plaza*
avenue	*avenida*
highway	*carretera*
route	*ruta*
street	*calle*
the supermarket	*el supermercado*
the tourist information office	*la oficina de turismo*
the train	*el tren*
I'd like to change some money.	*Me gustaria de cambiar un poco de dinero.*
I need a taxi.	*Yo necesito un taxi.*
Could you tell me?	*¿Podria usted decrime?*

I am looking for a...	*Yo busco...*
I understand.	*Yo entiendo.*
I don't understand.	*Yo no entiendo.*
Could you repeat that, please?	*¿Podria usted repetir eso, por favor?*
the exit	*la salida*
the entrance	*la entrada*
the map	*la mapa*
left	*esquierda*
right	*derecha*
straight	*derecho*
here	*aquí*
there	*allí*
east	*este*
north	*norte*
south	*sur*
west	*oeste*
birthplace	*lugar de nacimiento*
birth date	*fecha de nacimiento*
female	*feminino*
male	*masculino*
name (first)	*nombre*
name (surname/family name)	*apellido*
nationality	*nacionalidad*
passport	*pasaporte*
ticket	*tiqué*

Restaurants, Hotels, Shopping

I would like...	*Me gustaria de...*
Could you bring me the check, please? (*formal*)	*¿Podría usted traerme la cuenta, por favor?*
The check, please. (*colloquial*)	*La cuenta, por favor.*
a little	*un poco*
bill/check	*cuenta*
breakfast	*desayuno*
closed	*cerrado*
cup/glass	*taza*

dessert	*postre*
dinner	*cena*
drink	*bebida*
food	*comida*
fork	*tenedor*
knife	*cuchillo*
lunch	*almuerzo*
menu	*menu*
napkin	*servilleta*
open	*abierto*
plate	*plato*
spoon	*cuchara*
table	*mesa*
waiter	*camerero*
waitress	*camerera*
Do you have...?	*¿Tienes...?*
How much is it?	*¿Cuánto es?*
How much does it cost?	*¿Cuánto cuesta?*
Can I see...?	*¿Puedo ver...?*
I am looking for a...	*Yo estoy buscando...*
I'm just looking.	*Solamente estoy mirando.*
I like...	*Me gusta de...*
I don't like...	*No me gusta...*
Do you like...?	*¿Te gusta...?*
Do you accept credit cards?	*¿Usted acepta tarjetas de credito?*
Where is the bathroom?	*¿Dónde está el baño?*
I need a room for tonight.	*Yo necesito un cuarto por esta noche.*
single bed	*cama single*
queen bed	*cama reina*
What is the daily room rate?	*¿Cual es la tarifa diaria?*
bathing suit (*men*)	*traje de baño*
bikini	*bikini*
coat	*abrigo*
color	*color*
condom	*camiseta, condon*

dress	*vestido*
jewelry	*joyeria*
music	*musica*
pants	*pantalones*
sandals	*sandals*
shirt	*camisa*
shoes	*zapatos*
size	*tamaño*
socks	*calcetines*
suntan lotion	*loción de bronzeado*
towel	*toalla*
watch	*reloj*

Food

bean/beans	*frijoles*
beef	*carne*
beer	*cerveza*
beer (draft)	*cerveza de barril*
bread	*pan*
cheese	*queso*
chicken	*pollo*
coconut	*coco*
coffee	*café*
Coke	*Coca-Cola*
crab	*cangrejo*
egg	*ovo*
fish	*pescado*
fruit	*fruta*
gin	*ginebra*
ice	*hielo*
juice	*jugo*
lobster	*langosta*
meat	*carne*
milk	*leche*
nut	*tuerca*
onions	*cebollas*

orange juice	*jugo de naranja*
pepper	*pimenta*
pizza	*pizza*
pork	*puerco*
rice	*arroz*
rum	*rón*
salad	*ensalada*
salt	*sal*
shrimp	*camaron*
steak	*bistec*
	(could be beef, pork, or chicken steak)
sugar	*azucar*
tea	*té*
vegetable	*verdura*
vodka	*vodka*
water	*agua*
water (*carbonated*)	*agua con gas*
water (*still*)	*agua pura*
whiskey	*whisky*
wine (*red*)	*vino tinto*
wine (*white*)	*vino blanco*

Numbers

0	*zero*
1	*un/una*
2	*dos*
3	*tres*
4	*cuatro*
5	*cinco*
6	*seis*
7	*siete*
8	*ocho*
9	*nueve*
10	*diez*
11	*onze*
12	*doce*

13	*trece*
14	*catorce*
15	*quince*
16	*dieciseis*
17	*diecisiete*
18	*dieciocho*
19	*diecinueve*
20	*veinte*
21	*veinteuno*
30	*treinta*
40	*cuarenta*
50	*cincuenta*
60	*sesenta*
70	*setenta*
80	*ochenta*
90	*noventa*
100	*cien*
101	*cientouno*
200	*doscientos*
300	*trescientos*
400	*cuatrocientos*
500	*cincocientos*
600	*seiscientos*
700	*sietecientos*
800	*ochocientos*
900	*noveciento*
1,000	*mil*
one million	*un millón*

Colors

beige	*amarillento*
black	*negro*
blue	*azul*
brown	*marrón*
gold	*oro*
gray	*gris*

green	*verde*
orange (*fruit or color*)	*naranja*
pink	*rosa*
purple	*púrpura*
red	*rojo*
silver	*plata*
white	*blanco*
yellow	*amarillo*

Days and Months

Monday	*lunes*
Tuesday	*martes*
Wednesday	*miercoles*
Thursday	*jueves*
Friday	*viernes*
Saturday	*sabado*
Sunday	*domingo*
January	*enero*
February	*febrero*
March	*marzo*
April	*abril*
May	*mayo*
June	*junio*
July	*julio*
August	*agosto*
September	*septiembre*
October	*octubre*
November	*noviembre*
December	*diciembre*

Time

What time is it?	*¿Qué hora es?*
one o'clock	*la una*
two o'clock	*dos horas*
two thirty	*dos horas y media*

two forty-five	*dos horas y cuarentecinco*
	or *quince para las tres*
twelve o'clock (*noon*)	*mediodía*
twelve o'clock (*midnight*)	*medianoche*

The Vitals

bathroom	*baño*
Call a doctor.	*Llame un medico.*
Call the police.	*Llame la polícia.*
doctor	*medico*
drugstore	*la farmacia*
Help!	*Ayuda!*
I can't swim.	*No puedo nadar.*
medicine	*medecina*
Where is the bathroom?	*¿Dónde está el baño?*

INDEX

ABOUT THE AUTHORS

JONATHAN RUNGE is the author of 17 other travel books: *Rum &*
Reggae's Caribbean (2006); *Rum & Reggae's Costa Rica*, co-authored
with Adam Carter (2006); *Rum & Reggae's Brazil* (2005); *Rum & Reg-*
gae's French Caribbean (2005); *Rum & Reggae's Grenadines, Including*
St. Vincent and Grenada (2003); *Rum & Reggae's Virgin Islands*
(2003); *Rum & Reggae's Caribbean* (2002); *Rum & Reggae's Jamaica*
(2002); *Rum & Reggae's Puerto Rico* (2002); *Rum & Reggae's Domini-*
can Republic (2002); *Rum & Reggae's Cuba* (2002); *Rum & Reggae's*
Hawai'i (2001); *Rum & Reggae's Caribbean 2000* (2000); *Rum & Reg-*
gae: The Insider's Guide to the Caribbean (Villard Books, 1993); *Hot on*
Hawai'i: The Definitive Guide to the Aloha State (St. Martin's Press,
1989); Rum & Reggae: What's Hot and What's Not in the Caribbean (St.
Martin's Press, 1988); and *Ski Party!: The Skier's Guide to the Good*
Life, co-authored with Steve Deschenes (St. Martin's Press, 1985).
Jonathan has also written for *Men's Journal, Outside, National Geo-*
graphic Traveler, Out, Skiing, Boston, and other magazines. He is the
publisher and a partner of *Rum & Reggae Guidebooks, Inc.*, which is
based in Boston.

ADAM CARTER is a Chicago-based Cubs fan who spends his sum-
mers vending beer at the ballpark. While waiting for the Cubs to finally win the big one, he obtained a master's degree in International
Relations. Merging this background with journalism, Adam served
as the cultural arts reporter for a Washington, D.C. paper, *The Hatchet*,
and while working for the U.N, he traveled to Columbia to write articles about its internal refugees. His articles have been published in
Worldview Magazine and the *San Francisco Chronicle.* He currently
writes for *Filosophy Magazine* and is working on his first novel. Adam

has an unchallenged thirst for travel and has seen just about every corner, nook, and cranny of the globe. This is Adam's third book with Rum & Reggae; he co-authored *Rum & Reggae's Costa Rica* with Jonathan Runge and he was also a major contributor to *Rum & Reggae's Brazil*.

Leugim VIP Pub
Calle Luna

RUM & REGGAE'S
TOURISTO SCALE

1. What century is this?

2. Still sort of a secret; this place is practically empty.

3. A nice, unspoiled, yet civilized place.

4. Still unspoiled, but getting popular.

5. A popular place, but still not mentioned in every travel article.

6. The secret is out; everybody is starting to go here.

7. Well-developed tourism and lots of tourists;
fast-food outlets conspicuous.

8. Highly developed and tons of tourists.

9. Mega-tourists and tour groups;
fast-food outlets outnumber restaurants.

10. Swarms of tourists.
Run for cover!